THE ENGLISH SONNET

THE ENGLISH SONNET

BY

T. W. H. CROSLAND

*Assist me, some extemporal god of rhyme, for
I am sure I shall turn sonnets.*
                          LOVE'S LABOUR'S LOST.

TO
RAFAEL SABATINI

Out of old Italy, which was a flame,
A fragrance and a music, you have built
Empictured shrines of porphyry and of gilt,
Each of them lamped for damsel and for dame,
And for that Duke—the terrible of name—
Red as his bulls, or as the blood he spilt,
With Murder written on his jewelled hilt
And Glory laughing by the road he came.

Princes and Popes and Doges are for you,
And all their wild, sweet women—steels that rust
And loves that perished. Now in love and awe
Let us remember one who loved most true,
And, while the world flashed past him to the dust,
Set up, in Padua, his golden law.

T. W. H. C.

CONTENTS

Book I: The Sonnet.

	PAGE
I. THE SONNET	9
II. SONNET LEGISLATION	37
III. SEQUENCES AND SUBJECT MATTER	98

Book II: The Sonneteers.

SIR THOMAS WYATT	125
HENRY HOWARD, EARL OF SURREY	125
MINOR ELIZABETHAN SONNET CYCLES	125
SIR PHILIP SIDNEY	141
MICHAEL DRAYTON	158
EDMUND SPENSER	176
WILLIAM SHAKESPEARE	190
JOHN MILTON	227
JOHN KEATS	241
WILLIAM WORDSWORTH	250
CONTEMPORARY	272

NOTE

The main theory of the Sonnet set forward in the first sections of this book has not before been propounded. The theory as to the true origin of the Sonnets of Shakespeare is also new. The Sonnets printed on separate pages in Book II are the finest in the language.

T. W. H. C

BOOK ONE
THE SONNET

I

THE SONNET

IF jesting Pilate had possessed more than a reasonably sure eye for the enduring, he would have enquired, " What is poetry ? " All manner of tongues are busy with that question nowadays ; though one doubts if anybody really wants an answer. For criticism, of course, an answer in good set terms is best avoided, because the perfect answer defies contrivance, and criticism worth its salt can be as hard on criticism as *ante bellum* woman was " hard upon the man." Shakespeare, Milton, Keats, Shelley, Wordsworth, and perhaps Swinburne, Tennyson, and Browning are poetry, says criticism. They have the merit of indisputability and they suffice. For the public taste, one must do it the favour to admit right off that it knows, it knows, it knows. There is Rupert Brooke, *vice* Mr. Masefield, curiously dimmed by the war, coos the public taste, and there is the gentleman in the Sam Brown belt who wrote " My Pal

THE ENGLISH SONNET

the Baynit" and "It's Nice to do Fatigues on Mother's Birthday." These are poetry, not only at the bookshops, but in the abounding human bosom. The *Morning Post* and the *Daily Mail* have told us so and we are content. Criticism may be left to its own ponderous iteration. The public taste will ever be the sport and mock of circumstance—and journalism.

As for high poetry, the very phrase sets the shining intellect a-shiver. Except for purposes of friendly or unfriendly (and therefore always nefarious) comparison, there is no such entity. Yet of necessity the thing exists. Supposing that—with a view, say, of entertainment—we desire to acquaint ourselves with its definitions, whither shall we turn? Perhaps a poet of critical parts might serve us. Let us try Algernon Charles Swinburne—of the glittering pinion and very proud:

> Neither pathos nor humour nor fancy nor invention will suffice [to make a poet great]; no poet is great as a poet whom no one could ever pretend to recognise as sublime.

That is Algernon Charles Swinburne. Then let us try a critic of visionary parts, Mr. Arthur Machen, the apostle of "ecstasy" and

HIGH POETRY

the private rock and stay of minor reviewerdom : —

The most perfect form of literature is, no doubt, lyrical poetry, which is, one might say, *almost* pure idea, art with scarcely an alloy of artifice, expressed in magic words, in the voice of music.

We must take each of these opinions at its full value. Each of them is either the merest writing or an avowal of the faith of its author on a large matter. It is reasonable to assume that both are confessions of faith. As they stand they might be considered identical in meaning. But it happens that Swinburne puts his pronouncement, for a sort of text, in the forehead of a book which deals wholly and solely with the fellows of Shakespeare, that is to say, with the Elizabethan dramatists less Shakespeare himself, who is left out merely to make elbow-room for the others : while Mr. Machen nails Mr. Machen to the counter with this remark, " In a word, a perfect lyric, such as Keats's *Belle Dame Sans Merci* is *almost* pure soul, a spirit with the luminous body of melody." Plainly, therefore, the pontiffs are at a variance. Faced with an election of high poetry, Swinburne would have been all for majesty and might and mgnificence —" in a word " for sublimity ; and Mr.

THE ENGLISH SONNET

Machen, "in a word," is all for the "perfect lyric," *La Belle Dame Sans Merci*—"*almost pure soul, a spirit with the luminous body of melody.*" Choice between these two views, which needless to say are the typical views, and indeed the only possible views educible from the enquiry, might at first sight appear difficult. But deep down it is not so. Here are two lines of Shakespeare:—

> How far that little candle throws his beams:
> So shines a good deed in a naughty world.

And here are the twelve finest lines of *La Belle Dame* :—

> I met a lady in the meads
>   Full beautiful—a faery's child,
> Her hair was long, her foot was light,
>   And her eyes were wild.
>
> I made a garland for her head
>   And bracelets too, and fragrant zone,
> She look'd at me as she did love
>   And made sweet moan.
>
> I set her on my pacing steed
>   And nothing else saw all day long;
> For sideways would she lean and sing
>   A faery's song.

Now all questions of mood on one side— for high poetry is absolute and beyond mood—

HIGH POETRY

who in his senses can doubt which is the finer poetry ?—or which is, not "the *almost*," but the clear and sheer "pure soul," or "spirit with the luminous body of melody "? If it came to a matter of parting with the Shakespeare lines in their plain glory, or the whole of Keats's immortal bit of wailing, it is pretty obvious which should go. In the sacrifice of Shakespeare there would be unthinkable loss; in the sacrifice of Keats, no more than regret. On the one hand the spirit of man would be the poorer; on the other, only prettiness, sentiment, and virtuosity. In the Shakespeare lines you can find no trace of the fetches which are commonly and, if you like, legitimately supposed to make for poetry. There is no embroidery, no ornament, no fancy in the inventive sense of fancy; no word that of itself is "magical," no snare for the lesser emotions, and no striving after the achieved sublimity. Keats's lines, on the contrary, are a conscious cunning from the first word to the last, a studied and—if we may borrow a phrase from the reviewers—"amazingly successful" skilfulness, a triumph of craft.

> Her hair was long, her foot was light,
> *And her eyes were wild.*

THE ENGLISH SONNET

I set her on my *pacing* steed.
. . . .
She looked at me *as she did love*
And made *sweet moan*.

One sees at once where, and how, the jewellery was let in. Keats was too good a poet ever to have been under any illusion about this sort of thing. He would not himself have contended that *La Belle Dame* was more than a creditable trifle. If he had been told, whether by Mr. Machen or anybody else, that the lines were " *almost* " pure soul, pure idea, and so forth, and " the most perfect form of literature," he would have been amused. They are nothing of the kind. They fail of the seventh heaven; and this for a very simple reason, namely, that they are not concerned and were never intended to be concerned with that combination of poetry and doctrine —the phrase is Coleridge's —without which high poetry is an impossibility. The two lines of Shakespeare light themselves into the highest poetry, because they have a soul of doctrine about them. On the whole, therefore, it will be seen that we can depend more on Swinburne than on Mr. Machen for our definition of high and perfect poetical attainment. Broadly, we perceive that the

DEFINITIONS

sublime transcends the lyrical even in the Keatsean altitude of the lyrical. We perceive also that loftiness is an affair of the lambent intellect as well as of the great wing, and that the mere lyrical spirit, however exalted and however melodic, falls short.

Now what has all this to do with the English sonnet ? So far as one is able to discover the sonnet, whether English or alien, has never figured in the critical eye otherwise than as a form : a pattern, or mould, or set shape convenient for the expression of "intense but inexpansive" poetical emotion. " The small species of poem called a sonnet," says Leigh Hunt, who probably knew more about sonnets than any man before him. " The pint-pot of the sonnet," says a more modern critic. "A brief poetic form of fourteen rhymed verses ranged according to prescription," says Watts-Dunton. And by way of a real effort of definition by implication we have this from William Sharp : —

> For the concise expression of an isolated poetic thought—an intellectual or sensuous " wave " keenly felt, emotionally and rhythmically—the sonnet would seem to be the best medium, the means apparently prescribed by certain radical laws of melody and harmony, in other words of nature : even as the swallow's wing is the best for rapid volant wheel

THE ENGLISH SONNET

and shift, as the heron's for mounting by wide gyrations, as that of the kite or the albatross for sustained suspension.

"The sonnet has had many apologists," remarks the same writer further in his discourse. As a matter of fact it has had nothing else but apologists from Mears and Gascoyne down. Shakespeare himself, we are told, "unlocked his heart" with it; but he had gibes for the "key," even though he came to perceive that he might open the doors of everlasting fame with it : —

You must lay lime to tangle her desires
By wailful sonnets, whose composed rimes
Should be full fraught with serviceable vows.
. . . . . .
I had rather than forty shillings I had my Book of Songs
   and Sonnets here.
. . . . . .
And I'll be sworn upon't that he loves her,
For here's a paper written in his hand,
A halting sonnet of his own pure brain,
Fashion'd to Beatrice.

Straws, perhaps, though they show which way the wind blew. Milton, who brought the English sonnet proper into being, had so little respect for his instrument that he could use it for expressing himself "on the detraction which followed upon my writing certain treatises";

APOLOGISTS

and Wordsworth, who for his part lifted " the thing " clean out of its Italianate association and set it four-square on English ground past all dispute and for all time, wrote the perpetually quoted lines which, though defensively intended, are stark apology and sheer whimper.

> Scorn not the Sonnet : Critic, you have frowned
> Mindless of its just honours.

And he goes on to call it not only a " key," but " a melody," a " small lute," a " pipe," " a gay myrtle leaf," " a glow-worm lamp " ; after which " a trumpet " for " soul-animating strains—alas, too few," might perhaps be considered to fall rather flat ; and great as were his mind and perception, he could consciously and for himself get no more out of the " trumpet " than this : —

> Nuns fret not at their convents' narrow room,
> And hermits are contented with their cells,
> And students with their pensive citadels :
> Maids at the wheel, the weaver at his loom,
> Sit blithe and happy ; bees that soar for bloom,
> High as the highest peak of Furness Fells,
> Will murmur by the hour in foxglove bells.
> In truth the prison unto which we doom
> Ourselves, no prison is : and hence to me,
> In sundry moods, *'twas pastime to be bound*
> *Within the sonnet's scanty plot of ground,*
> *Pleased if some souls (for such there needs must be)*
> *Who have felt the weight of too much liberty,*
> *Should find brief solace there*, as I have found.

THE ENGLISH SONNET

In the lines italicised you have the sonnet, cap-in-hand. "'Twas pastime," "the sonnet's scanty plot of ground" "pleased if some souls ... should find brief solace there!" When the mighty conspire for belittlement, the less powerful are convinced. In all the literature of the subject you will fail to discover ponderable objection or argument which even begins to move the sonnet from its place among the suns of poetry; yet the accent throughout is one of condonation. " Please excuse her: she is only a little moon; the Lord knows wherein she hath sinned; but of your charity forgive her!" Very kindly, and doubtless because he had friends in the business, Watts-Dunton tells us that "the sonnet form" would seem to have had "a peculiar fascination for poets of the first class," and that it has "drawn" "some of the most passionate poets in the world" as "a medium of sincerest utterance"; but beyond this we are vouchsafed no glimmer of the actual truth. And it will be observed that even here the accent is the accent of caution and bland patronage. What is wrong with the sonnet that we should have a suggestion of the moth and the candle in that "peculiar fascination for poets of the first class"? Does one ever hear that blank verse had a peculiar fascination for Christopher Marlow,

DECASYLLABLES

or that four quatrains clinched by a couplet had a peculiar fascination for Shakespeare, or that chimes of rhyme had a peculiar fascination for Swinburne? And why shouldn't a passionate poet put his sincerest utterance into a sonnet, just as well as into blank verse or the lyrical stanza? There is no reason; and as a fact the reason of the whole matter is entirely the other way about.

And now let us hark back to high poetry. We have seen that the test for it is roughly sublimity. We say "roughly" because we are not prepared in this place to rule out of high poetry a few—very few—lyrical achievements which in parts, or more correctly flashes, are very nearly sublime. But we assert without reservation that if you take away from the fabric of English poetry those portions of it which may be properly described as belonging to the sublime, as distinguished or removed from the lyrical, you have taken away all that is greatest and finest. This is not to suggest that no glory remains; only that the remaining glory is by comparison minor. For reasons which have to do with pure poetics, it happens that practically all great English poetry has been written in decasyllabic lines. Sublimity in English climbs on decasyllables. It is attained for us mainly

THE ENGLISH SONNET

in blank verse; but also in the decasyllabic stanza — the blank verse preponderating. Blank verse worth talking about amounts simply to a succession of high poetic flights on the decasyllable, all making for nothing but sublimity. Poetry in decasyllabic stanza is either a succession of high flights, or an attempted long high flight, on rhymed verse instead of blank; the mark being still the same. And we say that the Sonnet is neither more nor less than a swift high flight at the identical mark, and on rhymed decasyllables instead of blank. We say further that just as the inherent spirit of poetry at its highest and noblest forces itself into the mould of blank verse or the decasyllabic stanza, so is it, on occasion prescribed by itself, forced into the mould of the sonnet, which is just as glorious, just as gracious, and just as free, powerful, and effective a vehicle for poetic utterance as either of the other two, and just as natural and necessary to be employed, on its occasion, as either of them. The notion that any great sonnet by any great poet has been written because that poet fell under the spell of "a peculiar fascination" for the sonnet form is, in our opinion, fallacious, and a mere putting of the cart before Pegasus. For the poet, it is the passion which searches

CHAUCER

out, discovers and lays hold of the forms preordained for its utterance and never the form that induces or sets fire to the passion. The whole history of poetry, both as a spirit and as an art, goes to prove this. It is indisputable that, in a measure difficult for an age with six hundred years of poetic triumph behind it to understand, the beginnings of modern English poetry, dating from Chaucer, were so many strivings and fightings for due and essential form. The struggle is usually marked to have been set afoot by Wyatt and Surrey, but for ourselves we shall set it back to Chaucer, and we shall say that it was by and through the sonnet, and by and through the sonnet alone, that victory became possible. It is true that no sonnet of Chaucer can be proved to exist. On the other hand, it is equally true that he was a poet, and that in his middle and most powerful period the influence chiefly at work in him was the influence of Italy. It is probable that he knew Petrarc and Boccaccio in the flesh. He was conversant with their poetry, and from Boccaccio, at any rate, he derived not a little of his subject matter. But it was the form of his Italian contemporaries that principally served him; and how are we to suppose that deriving from them the decasyllabic stanza and the

THE ENGLISH SONNET

heroic couplet and the new kingdom of expressional liberty those forms unlocked for him, he still owed nothing to the sonnet, which for prescriptive purposes was then as now ordered rhymed decasyllables in their finest and most convincing showing. On the " peculiar fascination " theory, Chaucer could scarcely help but experiment with the sonnet. On our theory his impulse, which was mainly for the narrative rather than the reflective, would not drive him into it, though he would of a surety instruct himself from its fluid effects and mounting sonorities. It has been said that Surrey was "the first poet to free the natural rhythms of English speech from the five-foot prison of the 'iambic' line." It must not be forgotten, however, that it was Chaucer who gave us that line, and that prison or no prison it was the formal foundation for everything of importance that came after. And we claim that without the sonnet the iambic line could never have been the instrument it was, even for Chaucer. When we turn to Wyatt and Surrey the significance of the form in its relation to the development of English poetics becomes clear and unmistakable. In their own day and generation these two writers wrought positive marvels for poetry, converting England into a verit-

THE FIRST BLANK VERSE

able nest of sonnetal singing birds, and making plain the road for Sidney, Spenser, Drayton, and Shakespeare. We must note particularly that Surrey, who with Wyatt introduced the sonnet itself into England, was also the introducer of blank verse. As far as is known, the unrhymed measure of iambic decasyllable in five beats occurs for the first time in a Provençal poem of the tenth century. The earliest complete work in the measure is by the Italian poet Trissino (1515), and it may be supposed that of this poem Surrey had knowledge. But it seems to us quite likely that the real source of his inspiration —and surely inspiration is the term—was the "blank" tercets of Petrarc. Here was Surrey, more or less "sonnet-mad," exploring and appropriating all that was finest in the Italianate sonnet literature, and particularly fired by the sonnets of Petrarc, the first tercets of which are commonly blank. He must have recognised, therefore, that the sonnet or decasyllabic line was capable of being handled without rhymes, and when he came to try his hand at that last ambition of poets who are not the greatest, namely, an English translation of the Æneid, the Petrarcan blank line was there for his purpose, ready and waiting to be seized upon and started on its career of wonder. Surrey

THE ENGLISH SONNET

put only two books of Virgil into blank verse; but they were sufficient; and the next blank verse was the flaming " *Tamburlaine the Great.*" Of the author of *Tamburlaine,* Swinburne says that he was "the first great English poet," " the father of English tragedy and the creator of English blank verse . . . as distinguished from mere rhymeless decasyllables." We can agree with every word of Swinburne's estimate without forgetting that Surrey, " the sonneteer," created for English the " mere rhymeless decasyllables," and probably had them from Petrarc. By *Tamburlaine,* of course —and as we contend virtually through the sonnet—English poetry came into its own; that is to say, into its full sweep and power of movement and its highest possibilities of flight. There has been nothing since to out-rival it at its greatest, and there never will be. And when you dig deep down for its beginnings in poetic, for the well of English not only undefiled, but of living water, there you find the sonnet.

Thus we come to the Age of Shakespeare and to Shakespeare himself. And looking into this marvellous period with marvels in it past count, we light upon a sonnet literature which would alone have made it a *sæculum mirabilis.* There are the sonnets of Spenser,

SONNET POETRY

the sonnets of Shakespeare, the sonnets of Drayton, each of them a poetry, and in the case of Shakespeare and Drayton, if not perhaps of Spenser, ranging with the highest. Sir Sidney Lee has counted " many more " than two thousand sonnets extant in the Elizabethan period. The bulk of them may be minor and negligible, but so is the bulk of all poetry at nearly all times. Yet the fact of their existence is important to a right understanding of the sonnet; because it proves, if proof were indeed needed, that when poetry flourishes, so flourishes the sonnet. And if you have a mind for the converse of the proposition, you may turn to the Augustans, the sonnetless Popes and Pyes, and the sonnetless Dryden; and even they could not have existed at all without the sonnet line. We need not, for the moment, deal with Milton and the great poets after him. One has only to say their names to call up forthwith assemblages of sonnets, each shining in its place like a galaxy, and each just as much part and parcel of high poetry as the best work in any other forms.

Without pressing the point too far, we might, indeed, venture the theory that a very large part of what is admitted to be the loftiest poetry belongs essentially and by its

THE ENGLISH SONNET

nature almost as prescriptively to the sonnet form as to the forms in which it is cast. Let us take at hazard some of the finest lines of Marlowe : —

> See where Christ's blood streams in the firmament.
> . . . . . .
> O thou art fairer than the evening air,
> Clad in the beauty of a thousand stars !
> . . . . . .
> Was this the face that launched a thousand ships
> And burnt the topless towers of Ilium ?
> . . . . . .
> Still climbing after knowledge infinite
> And always moving as the restless spheres.
> . . . . . .
> Zenocrate lovelier than the love of Jove,
> Brighter than is the silver Rhodope,
> Fairer than whitest snows on Scythian hills.
> . . . . . .
> Her silver arms will coil me round about
> And tears of pearl cry " Stay, Aeneas, stay ! "

What are these but the beginnings or ends for wondrous fine sonnets ? And there are passages in Marlowe which are nearly complete sonnets of themselves ; lacking nothing save due rhyme :

The first time when he pitcheth down his tent
White is his hue, and on his silver crest
A snowy feather spangled white he bears,
To signify the mildness of his mind. . . .

MARLOWE

But when Aurora mounts the second time,
As red as scarlet is his furniture;
Then must his kindled wrath be quenched with blood,
Not sparing any that can manage arms;
    .   .   .   .   .   .

But if these threats move not submission,
Black are his colours, black pavilion,
His spear, his shield, his horse, his armour, plumes
And jetty feathers, menace death and hell.

Two more lines and the rhymes, and we should have had here a great sonnet; that is to say, if the passage is great poetry, which, one takes it, nobody doubts.

Shakespeare, of course, abounds in similar sonnet stuff. We have already quoted " How far that little candle throws his beams, So shines a good deed in a naughty world," but what an onset or what a close it would have made for the fourteen-line flight! Innumerable other passages from the plays might be instanced, such, for example, as:

    Oh that this too, too solid flesh would melt,
    Thaw, and resolve itself into a dew.
        .   .   .   .   .   .

    No, let the candied tongue lick absurd pomp,
    And crook the pregnant hinges of the knee
    Where thrift may follow fawning.
        .   .   .   .   .   .

    When sorrows come they come not single spies
    But in battalions.

THE ENGLISH SONNET

There be some sports are painful and their labour
Delight in them sets off : some kinds of baseness
Are nobly undergone, and most poor matters
Point to rich ends.

. . . . . .

Night's candles are burnt out, and jocund day
Stands tiptoe on the misty mountain tops.

. . . . . .

    There is no woman's sides
Can bide the beating of so strong a passion
As love doth give my heart ; no woman's heart
So big to hold so much.

. . . . . .

O polished perturbation ! golden care !
That keepst the ports of slumber open wide
To many a watchful night !—sleep with it now,
Yet not so sound and half so deeply sweet,
As he whose brow with homely biggin bound
Snores out the watch of the night.

. . . . . .

To-morrow, and to-morrow and to-morrow
Creeps in this petty pace from day to day,
To the last syllable of recorded time ;
And all our yesterdays have lighted fools
The way to dusty death. Out, out brief candle !
Life's but a walking shadow ; a poor player,
That struts and frets his hour upon the stage,
And then is heard no more : it is a tale
Told by an idiot, full of sound and fury
Signifying nothing.

. . . . . .

SHAKESPEARE

    Here, here will I remain
With worms that are thy chambermaids ; O, here
Will I set up my everlasting rest,
And shake the yoke of inauspicious stars
From this world-wearied flesh.
  . . . . . .

His silver skin laced with his golden blood.
  . . . . . .

For God's sake let us sit upon the ground
And tell sad stories of the death of Kings.
  . . . . . .

    In such a night
Stood Dido with a willow in her hand
Upon the wild sea-banks, and waved her love
To come again to Carthage.
  . . . . . .

There's not the smallest orb that thou beholdest
But in his motion like an angel sings,
Still quiring to the young-eyed cherubins.
  . . . . . .

    'Tis better to be lowly born,
And range with humble livers in content,
Than to be perked up in a glistering grief
And wear a golden sorrow.

One is hard put to it to stop. All these beautiful familiar things, and literally hundreds of others as beautiful and familiar, have for our mind not only a surface relationship with the sonnet, but also a relationship which is deep and intimate and philosophically demonstrable ; as a fact we do not think it

THE ENGLISH SONNET

is possible to find either in Shakespeare or any other high poet at his highest a passage of beauty and power which runs to more than fourteen lines. Always they are decasyllabic lines, and always they could have been made into sonnets, and would have suffered nothing in the process. What is true of blank verse is equally true of the decasyllabic stanza. From *Lycidas* we take the following : —

>   Alas ! what boots it with incessant care
>   To tend the homely slighted shepherd's trade,
>   And strictly meditate the thankless muse ?
>   Were it not better done as others use,
>   To sport with Amaryllis in the shade,
>   Or with the tangles of Neæra's hair ?
>   Fame is the spur that the clear spirit doth raise
>   (That last infirmity of noble minds)
>   To scorn delights and live laborious days ;
>   But the fair guerdon when we hope to find,
>   And think to burst out into sudden blaze,
>   Comes the blind Fury with th' abhorred shears,
>   And slits the thin-spun life.

Another line and a half would have sufficed for the full-blown Miltonic sonnet, irregular as regards the rhyming of the first eight lines ; but otherwise fitting in with every essential of Milton's alleged conception of the form.

The same curious sonnet kinship is evident in the poetry of all the late moderns. Admitting for the sake of the argument that the sestet, or concluding system of a sonnet, may

FITZGERALD

with propriety contain a rhymed couplet, the following four verses of FitzGerald are nothing but splendid sonnet endings : —

> With them the seed of Wisdom did I sow
> And with my own hand labour'd it to grow;
> And this was all the harvest that I reaped—
> I came like water and like wind I go.
> . . . . . .
> [And] in the market place, one Dusk of Day,
> I watched the Potter thumping his wet clay;
> And with its all obliterated Tongue,
> It murmured—" Gently, Brother, gently, pray!"
> . . . . . .
> Ah Love! could thou and I with Fate conspire
> To grasp this sorry Scheme of Things entire,
> Would not we shatter it to bits—and then
> Re-mould it nearer to the Heart's Desire!
> . . . . . .
> The Moving Finger writes; and having writ,
> Moves on : nor all thy Piety nor Wit
> Shall lure it back to cancel half a Line,
> Nor all thy Tears wash out a Word of it.

From Tennyson, Swinburne, and Browning sonnet-matter is extractable in plenty. We give two examples of Tennyson, the first of which is nearly identical in form with some of the " iterated " sonnets of the Italians : —

> Now sleeps the crimson petal, now the white,
> Nor waves the cypress in the palace walk
> Nor winks the gold fin in the porphyry font,
> The fire-fly wakens : waken thou with me.

THE ENGLISH SONNET

Now droops the milk-white peacock like a ghost,
And like a ghost she glimmers on to me.

Now lies the Earth all Danaë to the stars,
And all thy heart lies open unto me.

Now slides the silent meteor on, and leaves
A shining furrow, as thy thoughts in me.

Now folds the lily all her sweetness up,
And slips into the bosom of the lake :
So fold thyself, my dearest, thou, and slip
Into my bosom and be lost in me.

Fourteen lines, you will note, and the last four have the force and clinching power which belong to the sestet of a sonnet. Then there is the never-to-be-forgotten " Come down, O maid," which might readily be transformed into two blank sonnets, and has a closing tercet such as only the proudest sonneteers can compass : —

Come down, O maid, from yonder mountain height :
What pleasure lives in height (the shepherd sang)
In height and cold, the splendour of the hills ?
But cease to move so near the Heavens, and cease
To glide a sunbeam by the blasted Pine,
To sit a star upon the sparkling spire ;
And come, for Love is of the valley, come,
For Love is of the valley, come thou down
And find him ; by the happy threshold, he,
Or hand in hand with Plenty in the maize,

TENNYSON

Or red with spirted purple of the vats,
Or foxlike in the vine ; nor cares to walk
With Death and Morning on the silver horns,
Nor wilt thou snare him in the white ravine,
Nor find him dropt upon the firths of ice,
That huddling slant in furrow-cloven falls
To roll the torrent out of dusky doors :
But follow ; let the torrent dance thee down
To find him in the valley ; let the wild
Lean-headed Eagles yelp alone, and leave
The monstrous ledges there to slope, and spill
Their thousand wreaths of dangling water-smoke,
That like a broken purpose waste in air ;
So waste not thou ; but come ; for all the vales
Await thee ; azure pillars of the hearth
Arise to thee ; the children call, and I
Thy shepherd pipe, and sweet is every sound,
Sweeter thy voice, but every sound is sweet ;
Myriads of rivulets hurrying thro' the lawn,
The moan of doves in immemorial elms,
And murmuring of innumerable bees.

There are thirty-one lines here, but we shall hold that the movement from the first line to and including the seventeenth is recognisably allied to the sonnet movement, and that the rest of the poem is similarly allied, while the last six lines, reckoned from "the children call," constitute a natural and powerful sonnet sestet, less rhymes.

It goes without saying that the theory hereby adumbrated is susceptible of easy challenge, particularly as it might be taken

THE ENGLISH SONNET

to involve the suggestion that any and all poetry in the decasyllabic line is virtually sonnet poetry. Our answer is that any indisputably great poetry in the decasyllabic line, and whether blank or rhymed, which may be cited for our confusion, will fall under one of three heads: unreflective description, plain relation or narrative, and sheer drama or exclamatoriness. For the rest, and it includes all the highest, we say it is sonnet poetry, and where there are rhymes, quite frequently indistinguishable from sonnet poetry. We shall depend for the security of our position a good deal more on the instinct and ear of the unbiassed reader than on the prepossessions and hard and fast conceptions of criticism. Let any such reader consider the passages we have quoted, or search out passages for himself, and compare them with the finer sonnet work, making due allowance for the absence of rhyme when it is absent and for its deviations from the stricter sonnet incidence when it is present. If he fails to follow us in our view, we are undone. If, on the other hand, he sees eye to eye with us, and we have faith to believe that he will, we shall between us have established a new claim for the sonnet which lifts it for ever out of the range of critical scorn and places the " apolo-

THE PROPER CLAIM

gists " at the serious disadvantage of having endeavoured to excuse the very pith and marrow of the stuff we call poetry.

To sum up we say of the sonnet:

(1) That it belongs essentially to the highest poetry.
(2) That it is the corner-stone of English poetry.
(3) That without it we should not have attained to the blank verse line, or the blank verse passion.
(4) That it is a form of absolute freedom for the very largest kind of utterance.
(5) That it is neither a convention, nor an arbitrary or pedantical contrivance.
(6) That when great poetry is being produced, great sonnets are being produced; and when great sonnets cease to be produced, great poetry ceases to be produced.
(7) That all the finest poets have been either fine sonneteers or unconscious workers in the sonnet movement.
(8) That there is no poetry of the highest which does not in some sort distinguishably ally itself with sonnet poetry.

THE ENGLISH SONNET

(9) That this alliance arises by the nature of poetry and not out of formalism.

(10) That fine poetry generally (excluding pure lyric) is identical with sonnet poetry.

(11) That there are occasions upon which poetry demands and insists upon the sonnet form as properly and imperatively as upon any form; and that when these occasions occur, and only when these occasions occur, great sonnets are written.

(12) That no great sonnet has ever been written out of a mere desire to exploit the form.

(13) That the "peculiar fascination" theory is fallacious and vicious.

(14) That the mean view of the sonnet implicit in such phrases as "that species of small poem," "the glow-worm lamp," "the sonnet's scanty plot of ground," and so forth, is an offence against poetry.

(15) That the highest poetry in English has been written only on three forms—(a) blank verse, (b) the decasyllabic stanza, (c) the sonnet.

II
SONNET LEGISLATION

IT has been commonly held that poetry is a law unto itself, and that there are no standards whereby it can be judged. Of the sonnet, however, this is certainly not true. The law has written itself explicitly and finally, and the standards have been set up and are irremovable. Of the law we may dispose very briefly. A sonnet consists of fourteen decasyllabic lines, rhymed according to prescription. Any poem of more than fourteen decasyllabic lines, or less than fourteen, is not a sonnet. Poems of sixteen or more lines are sometimes styled sonnets, but they have no right to the title. Any poem in any other measure than the decasyllabic is not a sonnet. For this reason, the poem which figures as Sonnet 145 in the Shakespeare Series is not a sonnet. Fourteen decasyllabic lines without rhyme, or fourteen lines rhymed in couplets, do not constitute a sonnet. The prescription for the rhymes of the English sonnet pure and simple may be formulated thus : —

a-b-a-b c-d-c-d e-f-e-f g-g

THE ENGLISH SONNET

And, strictly, the rhymes should be single, and never double. This form of sonnet was written before Shakespeare, but Shakespeare appropriated it to himself, and every one of his sonnets is so rhymed. Even in Sonnet 145 the rhyme scheme is maintained, and the sonnet "prologue" to *Romeo and Juliet* is similarly rhymed. The form is usually known as the Shakespearean. We call it the English sonnet pure and simple, because it was the first perfect form of sonnet to take root in the language. It is doubtful whether since the time of Shakespeare a really satisfactory sonnet in that form has been written. All manner of poets have tried their hands and their wings. Perhaps, with the single exception of Michael Drayton, they have failed, and Drayton may be said to have succeeded in only one sonnet. In a sense, possibly, we may regret that Shakespeare handled this beautiful form with such mastery; for after him, flight in it seems not only vain but presumptuous, and the most self-reliant poet will think twice before obeying an impulse which seems likely to result in "four quatrains clinched by a couplet." We imagine that if Shakespeare had written no sonnets, or only a few instead of a hundred and fifty-four, poetry might in the long result have been the gainer. The

THE MILTONIC FORMULA

Milton of *L'Allegro* could have done wonders with the sonnet in that kind, and so might Swinburne and Tennyson. But Milton was a wise poet. When his turn came to write sonnets he walked discreetly. Whatever his impulse may have been, he perceived that the linked sweetness finished with a chime was Shakespeare's and could be no other's. Therefore he fell back on the Italians, and out of them made an English sonnet of his own; writing just enough of it to tower, but leaving space upon which following poets might base themselves without impertinence. Hence, not only for the prescriptive rhyming of what we shall call the modern English sonnet, but also for the rough draft, as it were, of some of the more important laws of its structure, we must turn to Milton. For the first eight sonnet lines, the Miltonic formula of rhyme runs on two sounds and on two sounds only—thus:—

a-b-b-a   a-b-b-a.

This is invariable, and of course, a return to the *Rima chiusa* or close rhyme of Petrarc. For the last six sonnet lines Milton's formula is on two rhymes or three, collocated as follows :

       (1) *c-d-c-d-c-d*
or
       (2) *c-d-e-c-d-e.*

THE ENGLISH SONNET

There are variants, though not in the five finest sonnets. The Cromwell sonnet, for example, has the last six lines rhymed *c-d-d-c-e-e*; and in the Fairfax sonnet we encounter *c-d-d-c-d-c*, probably the two worst rhyme-schemes for the conclusion of an English sonnet that it would be possible to arrange. But in " How soon hath Time," " Captain or Colonel or Knight in arms," the sonnet to Sir Henry Vane, the sonnet on the Massacre in Piemont and the tremendous " When I consider how my light is spent," the rhyme arrangements are as (1) or (2), and it is reasonable to suppose that with the authority of Petrarc before him, and out of his own superlative instinct for sonority, he would know them to be the ideal and perfect schemes. With regard to structure, it is evident, both from the rhyme schemes and the general build of the major sonnets, that Milton recognised to the full the force and meaning of the Petrarcan sonnet " systems." According to Mark Pattison he " missed the very end and aim " of the Petrarcan scheme ; but with this we do not agree. Pattison and other writers after him have, in our opinion, been too quick to conclude that because Milton almost persistently violated the strict Petrarcan rule in a single, if vital, particular, he had no ap-

THE TWO-POEM "SYSTEM"

preciation of the rule itself. The rule to which we refer is, that between the first eight lines (or octet) and the last six lines (or sestet) of a sonnet there should be a definite break or pause in the melody and content, and that as the octet should consist of an enunciation of a complete poetic statement or series of poetic statements, the sestet, though arising out of and carrying that statement or series of statements further and to a full conclusion should have an independent beginning, clearly removed from what has gone before, but in the same train of thought. Let us take an example from Milton himself. Here is the octet of Milton's sonnet to Lawes : —

> Harry, whose tuneful and well-measur'd song
> First taught our English music how to span
> Words with just note and accent, not to scan
> With Midas' ears, committing short and long;
> Thy worth and skill exempts thee from the throng,
> With praise enough for envy to look wan ;
> To after age thou shalt be writ the man
> That with smooth air couldst humour best our tongue.

It is plain that in these eight lines we have a statement which is complete in and of itself. The lines might indeed stand for a complete poem, or at any rate a complete stanza of a poem. Excepting that the intellect might desire to have them developed there is no

THE ENGLISH SONNET

reason why anything should be added to them. The full period at "tongue" is not only natural to language and poetry, but natural to the thought. If the poem is to be continued it must be on a new effort of language and a new effort of thought. Consequently the sestet, though palpably arising out of what has already been said, will resolve itself into a new, if further, poem. Fully to bring out what we mean, we will print the sestet with a title above it :

To Mr. H. Lawes

> Thou honour'st verse, and verse must lend her wing
> To honour thee, the priest of Phoebus' quire,
> That tun'st their happiest lines in hymn, or story.
> Dante shall give fame leave to set thee higher
> Than his Casella, whom he woo'd to sing
> Met in the milder shades of Purgatory.

Here we have a second complete poem, of and in itself. Put together, however, the two short poems obviously make a much fuller and more complete poem than either of them by itself; and what is more, the intellect is brought by the second piece, taken as an addendum of the first, to the sure conviction that a poetical train of thought has been fully elaborated and properly finished. The intellect is accordingly satisfied and contented. It was more or less satisfied at the pause or break;

MILTON AND THE PAUSE

but at the end of the second piece it finds complete satisfaction.

Roughly, and for the present, this is all we need to know about the Petrarcan rule of the pause. It is a rule evolved, clearly, out of the *Rima chiusa*, which the ear proclaims to be complete when the end of the eighth line is reached; and to assert that a poet of Milton's culture and technical understanding set no value by it, or " missed the end and aim " of it, appears to us to be sheer nonsense; especially as in the instance we have given, he observes it to the letter. Now let us see how and wherein this the greatest master of high versification departed from the strait way. We will take his finest sonnet :—

> When I consider how my light is spent
> Ere half my days, in this dark world and wide,
> And that one talent which is death to hide,
> Lodg'd with me useless, though my soul more bent
> To serve therewith my Maker, and present
> My true account, lest he returning chide ;
> " Doth God exact day-labour, light denied ? "
> I fondly ask : But Patience, to prevent
> That murmur, soon replies, " God doth not need
> Either man's work, or his own gifts ; who best
> Bear his mild yoke, they serve him best : his state
> Is kingly ; thousands at his bidding speed,
> And post o'er land and ocean without rest;
> They also serve who only stand and wait."

THE ENGLISH SONNET

Where are the two poems or Petrarcan "systems?" Where is the natural break or pause? By strict rule the octet, or first poem, should end at "Patience, to prevent," and the sestet, or second, should begin at "That murmur, soon replies." And the pause should occur between them. But for the intellect the first poem ends at "I fondly ask," and the second begins at "But Patience, to prevent." So that in effect the octet is really half a line short, and the thought of the second half of the eighth line belongs properly to the sestet, while the pause falls in the middle of the eighth line, instead of in its proper place at the end of it. Yet it cannot be denied that there is a pause, or that there is a clear beginning for the second poem, which arises out of, and amplifies and develops the first, and brings the poem as a whole to a natural conclusion. It would have been easy for Milton to regularise this sonnet. Any poet of fair parts could, indeed, regularise it, without in the least straining, modifying or changing the thought and without detracting from the general beauty and grandeur of the sonnet as a whole. The line in which the fault lies is poetically the least essential of the fourteen. Why did Milton allow it to pass and by so doing mar the technical perfection of the piece? Pattison

MILTON AND RALEIGH

would seem to suggest that he did it on the principle of "Sheer ignorance, Madam!" Other critics, zealous to condone the faults of eminence, assure us that Milton admired, apparently to something like distraction, a sonnet of that great Englishman, but very middling poet, Sir Walter Raleigh, and that with Raleigh's sonnet for a model, the mighty-mouthed inventor of harmonies was hereby, and in other sonnets which exhibit the like blemish, reaching for or striving after a sonnet which, while moving in the Petrarcan framework, should be free of "the shackle of the pause," and shape itself as a continuous whole poem, rather than two poems the second of which should lend full and absolute completion to the first. For the theory of Pattison we venture to say that there are no tenable grounds. For the theory of the "continuous" sonnet the grounds are merely formal, and not intrinsic or actual. Milton's departures from the Petrarcan and natural rule amount to nothing more nor less than the overflowing or underflowing of the octet thought or content, and a consequent setting forward or backward of the true beginning of the sestet and the true incidence of the pause. We are of opinion that this poet, in common with practically every other English sonnet

THE ENGLISH SONNET

poet, save and except William Shakespeare who, as his hundred and fifty-seven sonnets prove, was a formalist of the formalists, suffered from that grave infirmity of sonnet poets, namely, a disposition to the tolerance of purely formal or technical lapses in their own work. We shall unfortunately be compelled to say a good deal under that head later. Meanwhile, and rightly or wrongly, we may assume that Milton knew perfectly well what he was about, and would not himself have attempted to justify his transgressions on the score that they were improvements or attempts after improvements. If ever there was a poet with an ear and an instinct surely Milton was the poet, and ear and instinct alike would tell him that octets half a line short and octet content running over into a sestet are not admirable, and that a close rhyme must be closed in the spiritual consciousness as well as by a sound. Consequently, and in spite of the apparent evidence to the contrary exhibited by the sonnets themselves, we assert that the Miltonic sonnet must be taken as an abiding precept for the formulæ which we have already laid down, and which we repeat for clearness' sake : —

OCTET : (*invariably*) a-b-b-a   a-b-b-a

WORDSWORTH

SESTET :
or
PAUSE
c-d-c-d-c-d
c-d-e-c-d-e.

Deviation from the octet rule is absolutely impermissible. Deviations from the sestet rule are undesirable, and when they run to couplets, final or otherwise, altogether vicious.

Leaving out Keats, who, notwithstanding the beauty and grandeur of a large part of his sonnet work, accomplished comparatively little for the English sonnet that can be considered to have been vital to its loftier development, the next great sonneteer is William Wordsworth. It is unfortunate that Wordsworth should have possessed only a limited conception of the importance of the instrument which he handled with such consummate power and large spiritual effect. We have already seen that for his poetic consciousness the sonnet was a minor and almost trifling affair. It is true that he wrote the two stock sonnets in praise of the sonnet; but in one of them at any rate his praise amounts to a sort of condemnation, while the condemnation in the other, uttered in the guise of a plea, will probably never be got rid of. And his

THE ENGLISH SONNET

feeble " Alas, too few ! " in respect of the sonnets of Milton, certainly cannot be echoed in respect of sonnets of his own. " Alas, too many ! " is the proper comment for them. Wordsworth was one of those sonneteers (also, alas ! too many) who simply would be sonneteering at all hours and in every condition of wind, weather and circumstance. A poet who could turn out a matter of a hundred and twenty sonnets under the title of *Ecclesiastical Sketches*, nearly seventy sonnets " dedicated to Order and Liberty," thirty-four sonnets concerning the river Duddon, and a sonnet miscellany of something like a hundred and fifty pieces, might seem to be past praying for, and particularly so when he introduces one of his collections with words like these :

During the month of December, 1820, I accompanied a much-loved and honoured friend on a walk through different parts of his estate, with a view to fix upon the site of a new church which he intended to erect. It was one of the most beautiful mornings of a mild season,—our feelings were in harmony with the cherishing influences of the scene ; and, such being our purpose, we were naturally led to look back upon past events with wonder and gratitude and on the future with hope.

THE MODERN SONNET

Nevertheless William Wordsworth was William Wordsworth, and though he produced sonnets almost by sleight of hand, so to speak, and greater in number than those of any English writer before or since, scarcely one of them is devoid of a sort of saving grace, some of them rank among the noblest that were ever written, and all are suffused with a peculiar reflectiveness, a still flame of meditative beauty that was new to literature, and new to the English sonnet, and that opened up for the latter fields of motion and rapture which had not before been invaded or attempted. We shall deal fully with this tremendous uplift of the sonnet in our chapter on Wordsworth, but for the present we may say briefly that more than any other poet he gave to the English sonnet its qualities of intimacy, poignancy and range of passion. And if his mind, as distinct from his genius, had been less pedestrian, less disposed to the banal and the inessential, he might almost have done for the modern sonnet what Shakespeare did for the pure English form :

> Dear child ! dear girl ! that walkest with me here,
> If thou appear'st untouched by solemn thought,
> Thy nature is not therefore less divine :
> Thou liest in Abraham's bosom all the year ;
> And worshipp'st at the Temple's inner shrine,
> God being with thee when we know it not.

THE ENGLISH SONNET

By the side of poetry like that even the Shakespeare sonnet at its highest seems humanly and spiritually awanting, and Milton in his might looks hard. It is the English sonnet *in excelsis*, at its topmost, and in its most passionate flower. While as a technician Wordsworth is frequently the chiefest of sinners and his form would seldom seem to be really perfect, excepting by accident, he nevertheless founded himself on the strict Petrarcan model, and in its totality, and notwithstanding its constant deviations from rule, it can be taken only as a further and final prescript of the true form, and it settles the scheme and system of the English sonnet for ever. It coincides wholly with the Miltonic sonnet as to framework; it removes the question of the pause beyond dubiety, and it fixes the whole structure as surely as the framework and structure of the earlier sonnet were fixed by Shakespeare. Since Wordsworth the technicians have taken the sonnet thoroughly in hand. There is no formal aspect, or attribute of it, and no refinement of its parts, that has not been exhaustively examined, discussed and put under a definite legislation. We are able to say of the sonnet what cannot justly be said of any other English poetical form; namely, that we *know* what it should be in its perfec-

STANDARDS

tion. Of no other form in English poetry can this be properly asserted. In spite of the range and vigour of our best blank verse, it is questionable whether we have even yet grasped the full significance of the measure. Marlowe gave it freedom and fierce movement; Shakespeare made it reflective and gracious; Milton re-invented it and put an august soul into it. But saving in so far as it approximates to the received excellence of these masters, we are unable to state with any certitude wherein its perfection lies. The later poets who have produced blank verse seem derivative when they write prescriptively, and feeble or repellant when they strike out for themselves. Who, nowadays, will approve the technic of the blank verse of Tennyson, except as to those passages of which it is the highest praise to say that they remind us of Shakespeare, or Milton, or both?

> It little profits that an idle king
> By this still hearth, among these barren crags,
> Match'd with an aged wife, I mete and dole
> Unequal laws unto a savage race,
> That hoard, and sleep, and feed, and know not me.
> I cannot rest from travel; I will drink
> Life to the lees; all times I have enjoy'd
> Greatly, have suffer'd greatly, both with those
> That loved me, and alone; on shore, and when
> Thro' scudding drifts the rainy Hyades
> Vext the dim sea.

THE ENGLISH SONNET

In its generation this and illimitable similar prosodising passed for perfect blank verse. Criticism applauded it; taste had it off by heart. Yet, by and large, it is the veriest butter-woman's jog-trot to market, a jerk and a jolt and little more than blank doggrel. Consider the ten low words which make up that dull fifth line, with its ignominious "and know not me" for the ekeing out of the beats. The only gleam of poetry in the passage—

> Thro' scudding drifts the rainy Hyades
> Vext the dim sea,

is unmistakably Shakespearean; though Shakespeare would have had nothing to do with "thro' scudding drifts." Between "the rainy Hyades" which "vext the dim sea" and the authentic "still-vex'd Bermoothes" of the *Tempest*, the difference is merely physical and not poetical. But for the one, it is improbable if the other would have done any vexing, or that the diction here would have been any better than in the preceding lines.

And who wrote the following, which we find on a considerable page opened at random?

> I had set my soul to suffer; or this hunt
> Had this despatched them, under tusk or tooth
> Torn, sanguine, trodden, broken; for all deaths.
> Or honourable or with facile feet avenged

THE DECASYLLABIC STANZA

And hands of swift gods following, all save this,
Are bearable ; but not for their sweet land
Fighting, but not a sacrifice, lo these
Dead ; for I had not then shed all mine heart
Out at mine eyes ; then either with good speed,
Being just, I had slain their slayer atoningly,
Or strewn with flowers their fire and on their tombs
Hung crowns, and over them a song, and seen
Their praise outflame their ashes.

Was it the adolescent Milton, preluding for his voice, as it were ? Not a bit of it. The passage comes out of *Atalanta*, and the blank verse parts of *Atalanta* are " perfect blank verse."

When we turn to the decasyllabic stanza, which again Milton revivified with *Lycidas*—this time after Spenser—we may read *Adonais*, and then the *Scholar Gipsy*, and then possibly Mr. Watson's *Wordsworth's Grave*, and we find the accent all of a sameness ; not copied, but learnt from the true formalist ; not imitated, but admirably and artlessly echoed.

As for the perfect lyric, we have already pointed out that for Mr. Machen, who is by no manner of means singular or unhappy in his choice, *La Belle Dame Sans Merci* leaves nothing to be desired. It happens, however, that the technical blemishes of *La Belle Dame* are as manifold as its technical beauties. " Woe-begone," " fever-dew," " manna-dew," " death-pale," and " hill-

THE ENGLISH SONNET

side," are, obviously, too many compound words for a " perfect " lyric of only forty-eight lines. Having insisted on the " theres " in stanzas 8 and 9, the artistry of perfection would have avoided the " heres " in 11 and 12. And right through the " lyric " there are too many " i " sounds—some of them villainously placed. It may be argued that we are hypercritical and finical. But this is beside the mark; the subject under discussion being perfection—the perfect lyric, or luminous soul of melody. A lyric flawed with superabundant compound words and a confusion of " theres " and " heres " is scarcely perfect.

> *I* met a lady in the meads
> Full beautiful—a fairy's *child,*
> Her hair was long, her foot was *light*
> And her *eyes* were *wild.*

Melody spoiled! And " why I " in the last stanza is cacophony. Further, one questions whether, on the whole and strictly considered, *La Belle Dame* can be a lyric at all. Lyricism, as we understand it, amounts to sheer singing, "pure soul" still quiring to the young-eyed cherubins. *La Belle Dame* partakes more of the nature of a rehearsal or a relation, than of a singing as by lark or nightingale. It is a little tale or story, magical and of an eerie sweetness; but still a little tale or story;

LYRICISM

a sort of pretty, short ballad in fact. For our own part, when we think of lyricism, we might recall the following snatches:

> Beauty falls from the air,
> Queens have died young and fair,
> Dust closes Helen's eyes.
> . . . . .
>
> Fear no more the heat o' the sun
> Nor the furious winter's rages,
> Thou thy worldly task hast done,
> Home art gone and taen thy wages.
> . . . . . .
>
> The stars of midnight shall be dear
> To her and she shall lean her ear
> In many a secret place,
> Where rivulets dance their wayward round,
> And beauty born of murmuring sound
> Shall pass into her face.
> . . . . . .
>
> Though one were strong as seven,
>   He too with death shall dwell,
> Nor wake with wings in heaven,
>   Nor weep for pains in hell;
> Though one were fair as roses,
> His beauty clouds and closes,
> And well though love reposes,
>   In the end it is not well.

Or this of Tennyson:

> Wild bird, whose warble, liquid sweet
>   Rings Eden thro' the budded quicks,
>   O tell me where the senses mix,
> O tell me where the passions meet;

THE ENGLISH SONNET

> Whence radiate : fierce extremes employ
> Thy spirits in the darkening leaf,
> And in the midmost heart of grief
> Thy passion clasps a secret joy.

Though we doubt if he be right, we are not now endeavouring to prove that Mr. Machen is wrong. Our whole point is that what may seem a perfect lyric to him or the next ecstatic judge, may be demonstrably imperfect, and perhaps other than a lyric in the strict meaning of lyric. In a word, we are no surer about the rule or law of the lyric than we are about the rule or law of blank verse, or about the rule or law of poetry in the decasyllabic stanza. For any of these it is impossible as yet to formulate fixed and stable statutes, the observance of which in the presentation of poetic content will result in perfection. Of course rules have been and can be put forward, but closely examined they will be found to be standards rather than rules—that is to say, if they pass, to any extent, beyond the obvious and the rudimentary.

For the Sonnet, on the other hand, the legislation is fixed, established, stable and unassailable. The observance of it means perfection; any breaking away from it means imperfection. We maintain also that this legislation, though supported and qualified

POETIC NECESSITY

by standards, is not even partially dependent upon them for its authority, but free of them, and based on the necessities of poetic and not on the arbitrariness of example. Indeed, as we shall show, nearly all the examples prove the rule by their plain defects. We hold that a great poet who had never seen a sonnet of Petrarc, or a sonnet of Shakespeare or of Milton or of Wordsworth or any other sonneteer, would in certain circumstances of occasion inevitably re-discover something like the sonnet form for himself; and the greater he was as poet, the closer would his sonnet conform with the established legislation. We have to presume that at the beginning the Italian sonneteers were virtually without models. As a form, the sonnet came their way by nature and instinct, just as the sonnet content came their way. There is evidence which might be taken to prove that Petrarc six hundred years ago had conscious knowledge of pretty well all we know about the sonnet to-day—less, of course, the special transfigurations of it developed by Shakespeare on the one hand and Wordsworth on the other. As regards framework, structure, system and movement alike, a fine modern sonnet is always a Petrarcan sonnet, and while a fine Shakespearean sonnet departs from

THE ENGLISH SONNET

Petrarcan type and belongs to a type of its own, the departure is not really radical and lies only on the surface. Perhaps we may say that the difference is as the difference between the note of sweetness and the note of mellow gravity blown through the same pipe. If this were otherwise we should be precluded from admitting that the sonnets of Shakespeare are properly sonnets. We should have to describe them as fourteen-line poems, akin to the sonnet, but not sonnets in the full and actual sense. Consequently, in examining the larger articles of sonnet legislation we must keep steadily in mind the fact that though the modern sonnet goes back for its essentials to Petrarc, it differs from the Shakespearean sonnet only in respect of rhyme arrangement and what we may term melodic tone, and not in respect of system or poetic principle. We have previously seen that the Miltonic sonnet, like the Petrarcan, consists practically of two poems, the later of which is the complement of the first ; that the first poem contains eight lines and the second six, and that there is a natural pause or break between them, and a clear beginning for the second or complementary poem. The sonnets of Shakespeare, in common with those of Milton, are usually printed without the typographical indication

SHAKESPEARE'S BREAK

of the break employed in the presentation of the modern sonnet. Nevertheless the two poems and the break, and the clear beginning for the second poem, are there. Almost any sonnet in the Shakespeare series will serve as an example. Here is Sonnet 28 printed with the break:

> How can I then return in happy plight,
> That am debarr'd the benefit of rest?
> When day's oppression is not eas'd by night,
> But day by night, and night by day oppress'd,
> And each though enemies to either's reign,
> Do in consent shake hands to torture me,
> The one by toil, the other to complain
> How far I toil, still further off from thee.
>
> I tell the day, to please him thou art bright
> And dost him grace when clouds do blot the heaven:
> So flatter I the swart-complexion'd night;
> When sparkling stars twire not thou gild'st the even;
> But day doth daily draw my sorrows longer,
> And night doth nightly make my grief's strength stronger.

Two complete poems, be it observed; the second complementary of the first, but beginning of and in itself. Palgrave prints Shakespeare's sonnets with three breaks, thus:

> They that have power to hurt, and will do none,
> That do not do the thing they most do show,
> Who moving others, are themselves as stone,
> Unmovéd, cold, and to temptation slow.

THE ENGLISH SONNET

They rightly do inherit Heaven's graces,
And husband nature's riches from expense :
They are the lords and owners of their faces,
Others, but stewards of their excellence.

The summer's flower is to the summer sweet,
Though to itself it only live and die ;
But if that flower with base infection meet,
The basest weed outbraves his dignity :

For sweetest things turn sourest by their deeds ;
Lilies that fester smell far worse than weeds.

On the face of it, such a division is prompted not by the sense and content of the poem, but by the mere rhyme scheme—three quatrains and a couplet. And herein, we think, Palgrave, and others with him, entirely miss the right meaning of the sonnet pause. It is obvious that the octet of the sonnet last quoted constitutes a poem to itself, and that the pause at the end of the fourth line is grammatical and rhetorical, and not for the intellect, which demands that the statement in the four lines should be completed and concluded. It is completed and concluded only at the end of the eighth line, and the pause at the end of the fourth is not only superfluous, but a positive blemish. So in the case of the sestet, or secondary poem, a conclusion at the end of the fourth line would have been lame and impotent, whereas by the conjunction of the

THE PAUSE

next two lines a full and effective conclusion is reached and the whole poem finished and rounded off. Therefore the pause in the sestet is also superfluous and undesirable. The only proper and necessary break or pause in the piece is at the end of the eighth line, that is to say, at the end of the octet. At the risk of iteration, we insist upon this point, because (after the rules as to the number of the sonnet lines, the nature of the line and the rhyme schemes) it is without doubt the most vital and important rule of sonnet structure, and failure to appreciate its proper significance —namely, that a sonnet really consists of two poems of a prescribed and fixed length, the one completing the other—is, in our opinion, destructive of both formal and poetic perfection. We recognise that the Shakespeare sonnets, as well as those of Shakespeare's contemporaries and predecessors, offer many examples of a subdividing of the octet or first sonnet poem into two more or less complete poetical statements of four lines each; but broadly and in the main, the principle is as we have stated it to be, and the exceptions or seeming exceptions do not vitiate it. Even as the octet of the modern sonnet exhibits a tendency to be divided into two distinct portions by the effect of the close rhyme, so

THE ENGLISH SONNET

the octet of the Shakespearean sonnet derives its tendency to subdivision from the melodic pause set up by the completion of the alternately-rhymed quatrain. It is to be noted, however, that this tendency would appear to be much more pronounced in the latter case than in the former, and hence it comes to pass that the frequency of subdivided octets is greater in sonnets of the Shakespearean mould than in those of the Petrarcan or modern mould. Before leaving this part of our subject we should note also that the so-called "clinching power" of the rhymed couplet with which the English sonnet pure and simple is invariably finished, has been greatly exaggerated by the formalists. It is true that melodically the final couplet has the effect of clinching or crowning the quatrains which have preceded it. Equally we may admit that the Shakespearean sonneteers regarded the couplet in the light of a kind of epigram which should drive home the poetic nail to the head; and frequently endeavoured to impart to it a separate and distinct force, removed from the force of the sestet. But, generally, we think it will be found to be a part only of the force of the sestet, and, for the intellect, not separate from that force; any more than the last three lines of a modern

THE FINAL COUPLET

sonnet are separable from the force of the modern sestet. The fact that in seventy-one out of the hundred and fifty-four sonnets of the Shakespeare series, the final couplet is preceded by a full period or the equivalent of a full period, and that these periods are demanded by the sense of the sestet-content in the whole of the seventy-one instances might be offered as evidence to the contrary. Still, we incline to the opinion that, on the whole, the force of the final couplet was intended to be melodic rather than material, especially as in sonnets by other hands than Shakespeare, too numerous to be counted, and not infrequently in Shakespeare himself, the final couplet is the least forceful part of the performance. The final couplets of Spenser and Sidney are seldom, if ever, stressed or insisted upon, and it is only by Shakespeare and occasionally by Drayton that any consciousness is shown in the matter.

We may now proceed to consider some of the theories as to the nature of the sonnet which have been set up by authority. It is first of all to be remarked that right down to the time of Wordsworth, the great sonneteers appear to have been content to remain in a woeful darkness with regard to the essential meaning and significance of the sonnet form.

THE ENGLISH SONNET

From Wyatt and Surrey to Keats the history of the sonnet is more or less a history of experiment. In three hundred years Shakespeare was the one sonneteer who did not swerve from the English form, and by an inflexible adherence to it gave it the definition and body which legislation demands. Michael Drayton, who, as we shall see later, was the greatest master next to Shakespeare, produced, in addition to his sonnets in the Shakespearean mould, a variety of irregular pieces which are sonnets simply in the sense that they were modelled on the irregularities of the Italian and French sonnet writers. Surrey, Sidney, and Daniel indulged the like taste for experiment. Milton, while observing in the main the Petrarcan rule, was no hard and fast stickler for it as regards at least one important structural detail. Shelley wrote a dozen sonnets, and to these perfection is the last word one would apply. Keats, though prolific and zealous in the matter of output, was either ignorant of the rule, or defiant of it. His sonnets are at once the admiration and despair of everybody who knows what a sonnet should be. By sheer force of genius he produced perhaps three really great sonnets; but even these are flawed, while the rest of his sonnet work,

LOFFT AND HUNT

though containing fine poetry, is past praying for in the matter of technique. Wordsworth was a bird of the same technical feather, attaining to perfection only by accident, and Coleridge, who talked and wrote a great deal about sonnets, as indeed about most other kinds of poetry, failed ignominiously whenever he essayed the form. So that while the knowledge that the forms of English poetic included a fourteen-line instrument of proved beauty and power upon which tremendous poetical work had been done, was fluid among the elder poets, none of them would appear clearly to have visualised that instrument, or to have been aware that behind its fourteen æolian strings and curious arrangement of keys, it had a soul or spirit peculiarly its own and capable of being comprehended and understood with a degree of sureness not compassable in regard to other vehicles of poetry. Although Leigh Hunt and Capel Lofft before him had pieced together the sonnet law, and made claims for the integrity and innate necessity of the sonnet structure, they did not travel very far beyond that. Both of them were too preoccupied with the example and too tolerant of the imperfect, the irregular, and even of the banal, ever properly to grapple with the

THE ENGLISH SONNET

true inwardness or heart of the thing. The tone of Capel Lofft is the tone of the collector and the expert cataloguer rather than of the lover of a poem for poetry's sake. He knew all about the sonnet, excepting that it is of its nature and essence a great poem. Leigh Hunt, on the other hand, though a trifle less chilly than Lofft, was little, if any, the less nescient, and reading him one might suppose, for all he hints to the contrary, that the sonnet—"that species of small poem"—is a sort of sublimated acrostic or exercise in *bouts-rimés* by the assistance of which many of "our most delightful poets" have managed to while away their half-hours of leisure between tea and dinner, or relieved the spiritual strain consequent on their more arduous and ambitious poetic performances. "A bright fire, a clean swept hearth and as much of the rigour of the sonnet as you may be disposed to put up with" is about the essence of Leigh Hunt. And this is not to throw discredit on his labours and learning or critical parts, but simply to say that for him, as for Wordsworth, the sonnet was the fourpenny-bit of the poetical currency, instead of the spade guinea. It is not, indeed, until we come to the mid-Victorians that the sonnet begins to be assessed at its palpable

ROSSETTI AND WATTS-DUNTON

and actual worth. And even with the mid-Victorians the re-discovery of its glory was largely a matter of fortuity; arising, at the beginning, out of an anxiety for the aggrandisement of certain *coteries*. When you say the name of Dante Gabriel Rossetti you say the name of the poet to whom directly or indirectly the modern English sonnet owes the very considerable share of critical *largesse* and patronage which has been bestowed upon it in the last quarter of a century. Rossetti's Italian parentage, and the trend of his genius in the direction of the decorative and the formal, may be said to have driven him to sonneteering as naturally as a duck is driven to the water. We shall not admit that he was a writer of great sonnets; but he was a great symbolist and a great formalist, and he wrote sonnets in quantity. And in any dictionary of biography you will find the late Theodore Watts-Dunton described first as " poet and critic " and next as " the intimate friend of Rossetti, William Morris and Swinburne." Whereby, of course, hangs a tale. We have never been of those who rated Watts-Dunton's critical gift too highly. That he possessed a critical gift we do not deny; but it is common knowledge that consciously or unconsciously, he consistently exercised it

THE ENGLISH SONNET

with a bias in favour of his "friends." It would not be unjust, even if it were unkind, to write him down for the King of the log-rollers. He had finer and more shapely logs to roll than ever fell to the lot of the come-day-go-day members of that wonderful craft or mystery, and he rolled with skill, assiduity and persistence. And with all his rolling he seldom failed to get in a good word or implication for the achievements or theories of Watts-Dunton. His article on the Sonnet in the *Encyclopædia Britannica* is a capital instance in point. The claims of Watts-Dunton to consideration as an authority on the sonnet arose out of nothing else but his friendship with Rossetti. Because Rossetti belonged to the Swinburne-Morris-Watts-Dunton "circle," and because Rossetti wrote sonnets, the importance of the sonnet form would be as evident to the Watts-Duntonian mind as the sun is evident at noonday. In entering upon the priest-like task of doing the best that could be done for Rossetti, the working critic and fugleman of the great Victorian mutual admiration society had necessarily to look up the sonnet and make himself acquainted with the learning on the subject. This he did, with characteristic and praiseworthy thoroughness. Not only so, but he ventured to evolve a

THE WAVE THEORY

theory of the sonnet which, while having all the appearances of universality, was really contrived to emphasise the particular excellence of the Rossettian product. The theory in question was called "the wave" theory, and by way of illustrating and giving it force Watts-Dunton embodied its principle in a sonnet of his own, which in his best pedestrian manner he entitled *The Sonnet's Voice: a Metrical Lesson by the Seashore*. *Qua* sonnet, the composition violates certain of the most elementary rules of sonnet construction. *Qua* gospel, however, it served Watts-Dunton and the sonnet critics of his generation very admirably. Writing on this subject, William Sharp goes so far as to asseverate that "what is known as the contemporary and sometimes as the natural sonnet [that is to say, the modern English sonnet] was first formulated [*sic*] by Mr. Theodore Watts-Dunton." And he adds, "With the keen insight which characterises the critical work of this writer, and that no less gives point to his imaginative faculty, he recognised not only the absolute metrical beauty of the Petrarcan type, but also that it was based on a deep melodic law, the law which may be observed in the flow and ebb of a wave; and indeed the sonnet in question was composed

THE ENGLISH SONNET

at a little seaside village in Kent, while the writer and a friend were basking on the shore." We have ever been suspicious of poetry which is deemed by its author or sponsors to derive an added interest or quality from the special circumstances of topography or companionship in which it was produced, and our instinct has not misled us in the present case. The octet of the *Sonnet's Voice,* or "metrical lesson by the seashore," runs as follows : —

> Yon silvery billows breaking on the beach
>   Fall back in foam beneath the star-shine clear,
>   The while my rhymes are murmuring in your ear
> A restless love like that the billows teach ;
> For on these sonnet-waves my soul would reach
>   From its own depths, and rest within you, dear,
>   As, through the billowy voices yearning here
> Great nature strives to find a human speech.

Now the whole of this octet is, in our view, as bad as bad can be. Whether in a sonnet, or any other poetry, but especially in a sonnet, " ear " and " here " are not tolerable rhymes ; " billows " in lines 1 and 4 coupled with " billowy " in line 7 has the effect of tautology ; " star-shine " and " sonnet-waves," that is to say, two compound words within the compass of eight lines, is infelicitous, as are, also, three uses of the present participle — " breaking," " murmuring," " yearning."

"THE SONNET'S VOICE"

Further, and what is more serious, the thought of the entire octet is confused, illogical and not true to the imagination, and the analogy and metaphor are clumsily put. The sestet which follows is equally faulty from the technical point of view, though clearer and better defined in its meaning. We are assured that "a sonnet is a wave of melody"; and that "a billow of tidal music one and whole" flows in the "octave," while its "ebbing surges" "returning free" "roll" in the "sestet" "back to the deeps of Life's tumultuous sea." In addition to the weak and hackneyed rhyming of "melody" with "free" and "sea," the sestet has the defect of containing a rhymed couplet, which is against the proper rule; and there is an abrupt pause at the end of the first line; a fault equally to be deprecated. So that one way or another this "metrical lesson by the sea" is about as complete a lesson in "how *not* to write a sonnet" as one could light upon. And herein, if you please, we have the initial formulation of the theory of the modern sonnet! We should have refrained from reference to this clumsy and reprehensible piece of work were it not for the fact that such meaning as it possesses has been employed as a working basis for practically all the theories of the

THE ENGLISH SONNET

sonnet which have been offered to us since the *Sonnet's Voice: a Metrical Lesson by the Seashore* swam into the critical ken. In his article on the Sonnet in the *Encyclopædia Britannica,* Watts-Dunton himself advances the wave-theory as a theory of importance without even so much as hinting that it was a theory of his own. He tells us that it found " acceptance with such students of the sonnet as Rossetti and Mark Pattison, J. A. Symonds, Hall Caine and William Sharp." " Symonds," indeed, he continues, " seems to hint that the very name given by the Italians to the two tercets, the *volta* or turn, indicates the metrical meaning of the form "; and he quotes Symonds as follows : " The striking metaphorical symbol drawn from the observation of the swelling and declining wave can even in some examples be applied to sonnets on the Shakespearean model ; for as a wave may fall gradually or abruptly, so the sonnet may sink with stately volume or with precipitate subsidence to its close." And, of course, " Rossetti furnishes incomparable examples of the former and more desirable conclusion," while Sydney Dobell " yields an extreme specimen of the latter " in *Home in War Time.* It need scarcely be pointed out that " this striking metaphorical symbol " amounts in

SUBSIDENCE

effect to nothing at all. Watts-Dunton might just as well have suggested that the sonnet "goes up like a rocket and comes down like the stick," or that it flies and returns like a boomerang, or that it swings out, pauses, and swings back again like a pendulum. There is no special harm in this "wave" or "flow and ebb" theory, excepting in so far as it may be taken for a justification of the irregular, halting and unlovely sestets in which Rossetti is so prolific and which the sonnet writers of his time, and since, have imitated with such persistence. What Symonds describes as "a stately subsidence" may or may not occur in certain examples of the Shakespeare series. We have tried our best to find an instance but without success; for when Shakespeare subsides, and he does subside at times, it is always in a manner for which "flat and unprofitable" is a better term than "stately"; and when lesser poets subside their case is no more to be admired. As for Rossetti's subsidences, they frequently amount to absolute topplings. Consider this for stateliness:

> But because man is parcelled out in men
> To-day; because for any wrongful blow,
> No man not stricken asks, " I would be told
> Why thou dost strike "; but his heart whispers then
> "*He is he, I am I.*" By this we know
> That the earth falls asunder being old.

THE ENGLISH SONNET

The italics are Rossetti's and not ours. While he was about it, he might have italicised those two " buts " also ; to say nothing of " by *this* we know *that* the earth falls." The abruptness created by " to-day " in the second line, and by the ill-adjusted pauses in the third, fourth and fifth lines, cries out against " flow and ebb " with a vengeance. Rossetti was altogether too fond of a sestet rhyme arrangement, which in our opinion can never be stately—*c-d-d-c-c-d* ; an arrangement whereby after the gravity and austerity of a Petrarcan opening one suddenly finds oneself tripping along to a conclusion on the tinkly couplets of Pope or Goldsmith. The subsiding wave of melody has forgotten its stateliness and taken to the light fantastic toe ; very nearly indulging, indeed, in the gay fandango. For the sake of discovering what form of a sestet it was that Watts-Dunton professed to find precipitate and less desirable, we turn to the Dobell sonnet. It should be observed that if our critic had wished to offer proper examples of sestets which are ungainly rather than stately, he could have found fifty to his hand by respectable poets who were his friends, or friends of his friends, or poets whose work is received as a part of literature. Yet he singles out Dobell and this sonnet of Dobell :

SYDNEY DOBELL

> She turned the fair page with her fairer hand—
> More fair and frail than it was wont to be ;
> O'er each remember'd thing he loved to see
> She lingered, and as with a fairy's wand
> Enchanted it to order. Oft she fanned
> New motes into the sun ; and as a bee
> Sings through a brake of bells, so murmured she,
> And so her patient love did understand
> The reliquary room. Upon the sill
> She fed his favourite bird. "Ah, Robin, sing !
> He loves thee." Then she touches a sweet string
> Of soft recall, and towards the eastern hill
> Smiles all her soul—
>   for him who cannot hear
> The raven croaking at his carrion ear.

Watts-Dunton must have been aware that this sonnet outrages pretty well every canon of the Petrarcan law. The rhyming of " be " with " bee " and of " hear " with " ear " offends past condonation. The sonnet has no system about it ; the octet content runs over into the sestet content, and for a crowning sin we have the final rhymed couplet of a Shakespeare sonnet grafted on to a sonnet which opens with close rhyme. By the use of " so " in line 8, after the " so " in 7, the sense is confused. How does one " understand " a reliquary room " as " (that is to say, in the manner of) a bee singing through a brake of bells ? The adjectival use of " reliquary " before " room " creates further confusion. " She fed his favourite bird. ' Ah,

THE ENGLISH SONNET

Robin, sing ! He loves thee ' " belongs to the sentiment of the very young laides' seminary. It would be silly in any sense ; in a sonnet worth mentioning in the *Encyclopædia Britannica* it makes one blush. Though the poem has a certain emotional power and poignancy, the total effect of it is an effect of amateurishness and ineptitude. It is almost as though Mr. Chesterton were to essay the part of Hermoine in the *Winter's Tale*. And taken as a representative showing of the sonnet form, it is calculated to bring sonnets and sonnet writers into contempt. Why did Watts-Dunton set it forward, not as a faulty, irregular and on the whole feeble sonnet, but as a proper instance of sestet subsidence not so " stately " and " desirable " as the Rossettian ? In point of fact, after the first few lines this sonnet is all subsidence, and it has no sestet content with a clear beginning of its own. The inference intended to be created, of course, is that any sonnet which does not conform with the alleged stately Rossettian sestet subsidence, is likely to exhibit the same technical futility as Dobell's. It would be just as reasonable to endeavour to prove that nine carat gold is eighteen carat by producing a piece of brass. Quite plausibly it may be argued that Watts-Dunton's comment on this

THE DESIRABLE SESTET

sestet refers only to the quick and startling turn of the thought after "smiles all her soul" in line 13. But he says distinctly that *Home in War Time* yields a specimen—" an extreme specimen "—of " precipitate " sonnet subsidence; and he quotes Symonds to show that similar precipitate subsidences occur in Shakespeare. The truth is that the sonnet does not subside, in any of the legitimate senses of " subside," and that no parallel or similar fetch to that here employed occurs in a single one of the Shakespeare sonnets. It is clear that by subsidence Watts-Dunton desires us to understand the stately returning sweep of a wave which has already spent its chief force. So that the most desirable form of sonnet sestet amounts to a reduction or tailing-off in the poetic force developed by the octave! Such reductions or tailings-off are only too frequent in the work of all manner of sonneteers, from the most eminent, down ; but to proclaim them for excellence is merely to flatter demerit. If Rossetti, who continually strove after what we may term a sestet " with a punch in it " (as witness the strained magniloquence of his final lines), had achieved his purpose on a convincing number of occasions, we should probably not have heard a word either about the wave theory or

THE ENGLISH SONNET

"stately" subsidence. And the sonnet would certainly have been no loser. If there be room for a wave theory at all, it might perhaps be better formulated thus :

> A sonnet should consist of two waves of emotion and melody, not fundamentally separated, yet each a distinct wave of itself. The first wave should have power and sweep, and the second wave, though of shorter duration, should have at least the same, and preferably greater, power and sweep. A minor first wave may be excused if the second wave is major. A minor second wave is invariably the result of failure of poetic force.

When a poet or his critics assert that a minor second wave is minor of a set purpose and for art's sake, they say the thing which is not. There has never been a poet born who will not make the second part of any poem greater than the first if he can ; and the sonnet form is virtually the outcome of the poetic desire for attainment on attainment. The octet may be likened to the seventh heaven, the sestet to the empyrean. The first atmosphere achieved, there should be poise ; and then a swift essay for achievement in the second. So much compassed, mortality can for the present do no more ; and the flight is finished —perhaps with something like :—

PERFECTION

      They also serve who only stand and wait.
or
      A sun, a shadow of a magnitude.
or
      Silent upon a peak in Darien.
or
      God being with thee when we know it not.
or
      I run, I run ; I am gathered to thy heart.

Any person who will say less for the sonnet than this, is no friend of ours. Out of the (probably) ten thousand sonnets which have been written in English, fewer than sixty can be accounted superlatively excellent, and nearly all even of these are more or less flawed, either technically or in some other respect. But from whatever point of view regarded, they are sufficiently perfect to stand for perfection, and their defects do not in the least reflect upon the sonnet as a vehicle for high poetry. The residuum is by no means negligible or base. We could easily assemble five hundred English sonnets, other than the finest, which have excellent poetry in them and belong to literature, if not to the highest sonnet literature. And for what would then be left, there is this to be said, namely, that its average quality both as poetry and execution transcends by far the average quality of minor blank verse and minor lyricism.

THE ENGLISH SONNET

Broadly, it may be asserted that there are no doggrel sonnets; though uninspired, unillumined and undistinguished sonnets abound. Even among versifiers who have no spiritual impulsion to the form—the pedants, the academics and the poetical daws who had fain be birds of Juno, there has to be some sort of poetic kindling or glimmering before the form can be attempted. By the mob of scribblers in verse, the poets' corner fillers, the passionate young misses, the soaring human spinster, the amorous retired colonels, the policeman, postman and potman poets, the yawpists, the banjoists and the patriots, the sonnet is eschewed; for the very good reason that it requires a certain amount of writing and takes up only a little print when it is written. Editors, good thrifty souls, do not encourage it, because "half a guinea seems a lot to pay for only fourteen lines," and when you say "sonnets" to a publisher you have locked him in his inner office for all time. So that the sonnet is unpopular in all the right quarters, and Parnassus rejoices accordingly. The which, of course, is by the way.

To get back to our theorists: after Watts-Dunton the field is almost wholly held by those critics or students of the sonnet who have at time and time written introductions

THE THREEFOLD ASPECT

to sonnet anthologies, or editions of the sonneteers; amongst them, Samuel Waddington, J. A. Symonds, William Sharp and Mark Pattison, and while three of these writers have accepted the wave theory and none of them has attempted to controvert it, each has done excellent work for sonnet exegesis and legislation. But, if we except Pattison, all of them appear to us to have erred on the side of the modest claim, and thereby greatly to have discounted such theory as they were able to put forward. This is especially true of Sharp and Waddington, both of whom while recognising the deep metrical and constructional necessity of the Petrarcan rule, still make great play with modern sonnet work which deliberately and wantonly sets that rule at defiance. Sharp holds that it is " well " to consider the sonnet " in a threefold aspect; the aspect of Formal Excellence, that of Characteristic Excellence, and that of Ideal Excellence," which, of course, is tantamount to admitting that any poem of fourteen decasyllabic lines rhymed after the scheme of Shakespeare or the scheme of Petrarc, or for that matter in any scheme which suits the fancy and convenience of the writer, is a sonnet and entitled to consideration as such. With this we disagree. We say that the

THE ENGLISH SONNET

principal test of the sonnet should be its structure in poetic, and that a fourteen line poem in decasyllables, however so strictly rhymed, is not a sonnet unless the octet and the sestet are so distinguishably separable as to constitute independent (though related) poems of and in themselves. Thus, from our point of view, the fourteen-line poem of Dobell, previously quoted, is no more a sonnet than if it had been written in rhymed couplets throughout, and this for the reason that its octet and sestet exist only as matters of rhyme arrangement and not as matters of organic structure. Thus when Sharp includes Dobell's fourteen-line poem in his *Sonnets of the Nineteenth Century*, which he does, he is including something which is not a sonnet, and has no right to consideration as a sonnet whether of the nineteenth or any other century. And the sonnet in question is not by any means the only piece of decasyllabic metricism which wrongfully figures in Sharp's collection, and the whole of the other collections we have seen are similarly marred. It will be urged that such a principle of exclusion rules out of sonnet literature much excellent, and it may even be, transcendent poetry, which is commonly and authoritatively accepted as sonnet-poetry. To which our reply is: so

THE MARCH OF POETRY

much the better for the sonnet, not only as a thing accomplished, but also as a thing yet to be accomplished. Poetry itself could suffer nothing by the operation of this principle; the sonnet would be a distinct gainer. If there be anything in high poetry at all, we have no right to assume that it has come to the end of its flowering and will never bloom powerfully again. As the world grows older, we believe the tendency is for it to grow more spiritually-minded. For one person who read poetry in Shakespeare's time probably fifty read it to-day, and in that estimate we make due allowance for differences of population and education. And for one poet of the spacious times of Queen Elizabeth there are a good six poets in the still more spacious times into which through war and travail we are just beginning to enter. It is heresy to say that we shall ever again produce a poet of Shakespeare's stature, but we have faith that when the spirit of man comes really to need such another, he will be there. And we have always to remember that it is not alone the giants who have created the fabric of English literature. Lesser poets have helped, and lesser poets are still helping. The poets of our own time may perhaps best be described as "a fair to middling lot," but we question

THE ENGLISH SONNET

whether there is a single one of them who has failed, or can fail, to produce something (however seemingly unimportant in cautious eyes) that men will not willingly let die. And as the proverb hath it, " Many a mickle makes a muckle." What is true of poetry generally is also true of sonnet poetry, and particularly of our later sonnet poetry, which has to a great extent been written by men (and women) who do not figure in the public eye as terrific or abounding poets, and can yet boast of a certain amount of proud achievement. We think that this achievement is not by any means at its period, and that we are on the threshold of still greater accomplishment; and we say this in face of the fact that the output of really fine sonnets in late years has been exiguous : How comes it to pass that while beautiful sonnets can be and are being produced by contemporary poets, the number of them is so few ? The answer is : because the modern poets, like the older poets, labour under the gravest misapprehension as to the nature and range of the form and that they are confirmed in these misapprehensions by the tolerances and compromises of sonnet criticism. We have remarked on the inclusion of Dobell's fourteen-line poem in what purports to be a representative assemblage of

IRREGULARISTS

nineteenth-century sonnets. It would be interesting to know under which of Sharp's aspects of excellence, formal, characteristic or ideal, it found inclusion. Formally, it is impossible; characteristic, it may conceivably be, though Dobell proved himself capable of better work; ideal, it certainly is not. The truth is doubtless that it was put in simply because in his day Dobell had a vogue. We do not deny that it is a pretty and moving poem. Our point is that it is not a sonnet, and has no title so to be called. And the fact of its inclusion seems to show that Sharp was willing to admit into the kingdom of the sonnet, work which, while falling short of all three of the qualities of excellence upon which he proposes to base judgment, might yet appear to have vestiges of some of them. Such a theory of the sonnet makes a mock of the legislation, and is destructive of the principles upon which a sound view of the sonnet must be built. If *Home in War Time* is a sonnet, then all manner of other and greater pieces in the decasyllabic line are sonnets. Here, for ex-example, is Milton, on "the admirable dramatic poet, W. Shakespeare":

> What needs my Shakespeare for his honour'd bones,
> The labour of an age in piled stones?

THE ENGLISH SONNET

Or that his hallow'd reliques should be hid
Under a starry-pointing pyramid ?
Dear son of memory, great heir of fame,
What need'st thou such weak witness of thy name ?
Thou in our wonder and astonishment
Hast built thyself a live-long monument.

For whilst to th' shame of slow-endeavouring art
Thy easy numbers flow, and that each heart
Hath from the leaves of thy unvalued book
Those Delphic lines of deep impression took,
Then thou our fancy of itself bereaving,
Dost make us marble with too much conceiving ;
And so sepúlchred in such pomp dost lie,
That kings for such a tomb would wish to die.

Why is a poem like that excluded from sonnet-literature, what time the Dobells and the Ebenezer Elliots, and the William Allinghams and the Watts-Duntons of this world have their fourteen-line pribbles and prabbles and palterings held up for our admiration as sonnets ? " Oh," it may be answered, "but there are sixteen lines in Milton's Shakespeare poem, and it is written in rhymed couplets, and Milton himself never called it a sonnet, and neither has anybody else. One must draw the line somewhere ; and you cannot claim all the fine poetry for sonnets." Well, we contend that structurally this poem approximates much more nearly to the sonnet than Dobell's. It is fashioned on the two-poem system of

SINNERS

Petrarc and Shakespeare. It has sixteen lines, but so had some of the sonnets of Surrey, Sydney, Daniel, and Drayton. It is in rhymed couplets—and there's the rub. We have just sonnet-sense enough to put up the *chevaux-de-frise* against rhymed couplets!

But we have not sonnet-sense (or is it pluck?) enough to put up the bar against countless deformities, abnormalities, irregularities, bastardies, impertinencies and fatuities which grin at us from quite half of the pages of any sonnet anthology we care to turn over. Anything in the shape of fourteen-line decasyllabics (other than rhymed couplets) that a poet of standing, and even of no standing at all, cares to throw together and dub " sonnet," is a sonnet, an English sonnet and nothing else but a sonnet. Rossetti's glib sestet couplets must be forgiven him :

> Yon thicket's breath—can that be eglantine ?
> Those birds—can they be morning's chorister ?
> Can this be earth ? Can these be banks of furze ?

must be admired. Coleridge may rhyme " I," " lie," " piety " and " perplexity," and stick a Shakespearean sestet on a Petrarcan octet, and still have " only just missed writing [a sonnet] of supreme excellence " ; William Lisle Bowles can indulge the like sin and

THE ENGLISH SONNET

survive ; because Coleridge by some unaccountable Homeric nodding, praised him. And of these laches, and a wilderness of worse ones, so little note is taken by the critical that they pass for currency, and are even extolled for merit and held forward as models and "authority." A while ago we had occasion to reprove a "famous critic" for putting couplets into the sestet of a sonnet. His answer was, not that the law of the modern sonnet permitted it, but that he had the authority of Swinburne and Rossetti to justify him. Thus are the lapses of genius made out to be exemplary.

We shall now endeavour to set down for the benefit of whom it may concern a complete canon of the modern English sonnet. The rules in italic are imperative ; those in Roman type are essential to perfection.

(1) *The sonnet must consist of fourteen decasyllabic (Iambic) lines.*

(2) *It must be rhymed in two systems,* (a) *the* Octet, *or first eight lines;* (b) *the* Sestet, *or last six lines.*

(3) *In the octet, the first, fourth, fifth and eighth lines must rhyme together, and the second, third, sixth and seventh must rhyme together.*

THE CANON

(4) *The sestet may be on two rhymes or three, that is to say, the first, third and fifth lines must rhyme together, and the second, fourth and sixth ; or the first, second and third with the third, fourth and fifth.*

(5) Words ending in " ty," " ly " and " cy " must not be used as rhymes whether in octet or sestet. This also applies to the pronoun " I " and to easy or over-worked rhymes such as " see," " me," " be " and " day," " may " " play." " Be," " bee," " maybe," " sea," " see " and words ending in " cy " do not rhyme together, and must not be " rhymed " in either octet or sestet.

(6) *No sestet should contain a rhymed couplet or couplets, and a sestet may not end with a rhymed couplet.* The reason for this is, that what virtually amount to three rhymed couplets have already been used in the octet, and a further couplet or couplets in the sestet thus become monotonous. *The final rhymed couplet belongs exclusively to the Shakespearean sonnet and must not be used in a modern English sonnet in any circumstances.*

THE ENGLISH SONNET

(7) The two rhymes of the octet must be on different combinations of consonants as well as on different vowel sounds. Thus a quatrain rhymed "sedge," "dodge," "lodge," "wedge," is as impermissible as a quatrain rhymed "brain," "rain," "wain," "fain."

(8) Rhymes of the sestet must not be on the same combination of consonants nor on the same vowel sounds as those in the octet. Therefore if "fist," "brave," "drave" "mist" have been used in the octet, "list," "gave," "wist," "save," "twist," "nave" must not appear in the sestet, nor must such rhymes appear even with a previously unused rhyme sound between them. The reason here, again, is the avoidance of monotony.

(9) Double rhymes are best avoided altogether; but if used in an octet, they should not be repeated in a sestet, and a sestet with double rhymes should not be preceded by an octet with double rhymes. Mark Pattison holds that double rhymes are inadmissible, but we should not lay this down for

THE CANON

a hard and fast rule, though we think that if used, they should be used very sparingly.

(10) The fourteen lines of a sonnet may be absolutely smooth and equable, or they may contain an occasional elision or redundant syllable. They should be ruled rather by accent than by mere beat, but in no case may there be a line or lines which cannot be *read* as decasyllabic without difficulty or hesitation.

(11) Full pauses should never be employed after the first word in a line, or at the end of the first, second, third, fifth, sixth or seventh line of the octet, or at the end of the first or fifth line of the sestet.

(12) More than one full period in a single line, or more than two or three full periods, or colon pauses placed elsewhere than at the ends of lines, are a defect.

(13) *While the sonnet must have unity, there must be a clear break between the octet and the sestet.* It has been held that the thought or mood should be led up to or opened in the first four lines of

THE ENGLISH SONNET

the octet and fully unfolded by the second four lines. There is nothing against this alleged rule, but failure definitely to observe the first part of it cannot be considered a blemish. Failure to observe the second part of it, however, is a serious blemish. There are occasions upon which the octet content may be allowed to overflow into the first line of the sestet; *but such overflow should never take up more than a part of the first sestet line. When the octet content overflows into the second line of the sestet, the proper sonnet system begins to be destroyed, while a poem in which the octet content is carried further than the second line of the sestet ceases to be a sonnet.*

(14) *The sestet of a sonnet should have a clear and independent beginning of its own and constitute a separate short poem of and in itself, though arising out of, developing and bringing to a full conclusion the first or octet-poem. The sestet should never be inferior in force or beauty to the octet,* and preferably it should excel the octet in these regards. It need not, however, and indeed should not in-

THE CANON

variably be at its loftiest in the final line, which must not suggest strain or magniloquence on the one hand, nor have the effect of epigram on the other.

(15) *There can be only one legitimate break or turn or pause in a sonnet, namely, that between the octet and the sestet.* The breaking up of the octet into two separate poems by its quatrains, and of the sestet into two separate poems by its tercets, cannot be countenanced, at any rate in one and the same sonnet.

(16) *The subject matter of a sonnet must be emotional or reflective, or both.* Mere descriptions of scenery, or recitals of events, or laudations of the beauty of persons, however admirably done, are not sufficient. They may be used for the content of the octet; but in the sestet following such octet content there must be developed a passion or emotion sufficient to lift the poem as a whole out of the region of word-painting into that of exalted poetry.

Sonnets have been written with the

THE ENGLISH SONNET

avowed purpose of creating sheer music and beauty, free of appeal to the emotions or moral nature. Objection is taken to these on the ground that they are deficient in doctrinal suggestion or quality. We agree up to a point. At the same time it seems probable that beauty, beautifully expressed, has a doctrinal force, and when they are not too fantastically conceived, which is their common demerit, exercises in this kind may attain marked excellence.

A kind of sonnet of description and observation combined with humorous or cynical commentary has been put forward by certain modern writers. It is clear that such sonnets can in no circumstances amount to high poetry, and therefore, while sometimes entertaining, they are negligible as contributions to sonnet-literature.

(17) A sonnet must not be dramatic or exclamatory in its diction; it must not be overburdened with interrogative lines or sentences; it must not contain quotations from other sonnets or other poems; it must not begin or end with a Christian name and sur-

THE CANON

name; it must be in English throughout and entirely free from slang, cant, and foreign words and phrases, Americanisms, dialect, Greek, Latin, Romany, uncouth place-names; technical and scientific nomenclature, and names with unpoetic associations, such as " gramaphone," " telephone," " cinematograph."

(18) It must also be free from split infinitives, compound words, italicised words or phrases, words or phrases in capital letters (other, of course, than the personal pronoun " I," which, again, must be used sparingly); inverted sentences, phrases and sentences in which words are obviously removed from their natural places in order to eke out rhyme or measure; iterations of the possessive pronoun "my," or of the particles, or of the same conjunction; and it should not have too many lines beginning with " and."

(19) The precise poetic meaning of every word and phrase must be clear and unambiguous; there must be no confusion or obscurity of thought or idea; the metaphors, similies, and

THE ENGLISH SONNET

analogies must be true for the imagination; ornament must not be obtruded; the symbolism must at least have the appearance of freshness; the " fancy " must not be far-fetched or over-elaborated, and mere " conceits " must be avoided.

(20) It has been pointed out by Wordsworth that a large part of the language of poetry does not differ from the language of prose; and this dictum is often set up as an excuse for uninspired metrical writing. Obviously, however, the shorter the poem the less apparent should be its prosaisms, and in a sonnet they should not be apparent at all.

(21) By the processes of time and the operation of accident English words and phrases and idioms which are perfectly sound of themselves occasionally become degraded or vulgarised. When this has happened such words, phrases or idioms should not be employed in a sonnet. As an example of what we mean, we may take the last line of Shakespeare's sonnet, 144 :

> Till my bad angel fire my good one out.

Since Shakespeare's day, to " fire out "

THE CANON

has acquired a vulgar, comic or burlesque meaning. So that in sonnets angels good or bad can no longer " fire out." Another instance is the adjective " glad "—a fine poetic word, which, however, can be no longer prefixed to " eye " or " hand," because " glad eye " and " glad hand " are now vulgar expressions. Even statements which remotely suggest, or are calculated to recall such vulgarisms, must be avoided in a sonnet. " Thy feet are cold," for example, will not do, because it might suggest the cant phrase " cold feet." It is presumed, of course, that the reader of sonnets has not " come to mock," but he has a right to expect that he will not be given verbal invitations to mockery.

Many of the foregoing rules will appear so obvious that it may be considered superfluous to set them out. Yet there is not a single one of them which has not been violated by the sonneteers. Quite outside all questions of metricism and poetic, we must remember that anything which is bad in prose is bad in poetry, and anything which is bad in poetry is unpardonable in the sonnet.

III

SEQUENCES AND SUBJECT MATTER

THERE remain for our consideration a variety of incidental matters which, if they do not materially concern us in a large view of the sonnet, may nevertheless require to be discussed. The first and most important of them is the question of the sonnet sequence. Historically the sonnet may be said almost to have its foundation in the sequence. The sonneteers down to Shakespeare wrote sequences and virtually nothing but sequences. Outside the sequence Shakespeare wrote only the solitary sonnet prologue to which we have previously referred. It is evident, therefore, that in the minds of these earlier poets the sonnet was regarded as a form which demanded to be written in sequences. The sequence was a fashion amongst them, and, perhaps, a law. Although they wrote sonnets of single and perfect beauty, the aim was to build ponderable monuments with them. The parts were polished and finished, but it was to the whole

IMMORTALITY

that the sonnet-poet looked for his principal effect and for his fame.

> Not marble and not gilded monuments
> Of Princes, shall outlive this powerful rhyme,

prophesied Shakespeare.

> Ensuing ages yet my rimes shall cherish
> Where I entomb'd, my better part shall save ;
> And though this earthly body fade and die
> My name shall mount upon eternity,

sings Drayton. Not to be outdone, Spenser boasts of " this verse, that never shall expire " ; and while Sidney says

> Nor so ambitious am I, as to frame
> A nest for my young praise in laurel tree ;
> In truth, I swear I wish not there should be
> Graved in my epitaph a Poet's name,

it is only after expressing the " highest wish " that the " highway " of love may be kissed by his inamorata's feet for " hundreds of years," which is a diffident method of indulging the sequence writer's fixed belief in the durable quality of his poetry. And the dream of each of these poets has come true. But there is this also to be noted in respect of all of them: namely, that in the main their threads of sequence are extremely thin, and slight, the " story," such as it is, being unfolded by a sequence of mood rather than of events; and that the collocation might

THE ENGLISH SONNET

be in a greater or less degree waived without serious loss to the total beauty of the work. In the whole of these sequences one finds only here and there a sonnet which is really dependent for its thought and meaning, upon anything that has gone before. That is to say, the sequences develop or advance no argument, and no story which is definitely related. Even the inglorious tale which Shakespeare is held to unfold comes to us more through inference than direct or explicit relation. As an example in point let us take the two following sonnets of Spenser.

> Ah, why hath nature to so hard a heart
> Given so goodly gifts of beauty's grace,
> Whose pride depraves each other better part,
> And all those precious ornaments deface?
> Sith to all other beasts of bloody race
> A dreadful countenance she given hath:
> That with their terror all the rest may chase,
> And warn to shun the danger of their wrath.
> But my proud one doth work the greater scath
> Through sweet allurement of her lovely hue,
> That she the better may in bloody bath
> Of such poor thralls her cruel hands embrew.
> But did she know how ill these two accord
> Such cruelty she would have soon abhorr'd.

> My love is like to ice and I to fire;
> How comes it then that this her cold so great,
> Is not dissolv'd through my so hot desire,
> But harder grows the more I her intreat?

SEQUENCE

Or how comes it that my exceeding heat
Is not delayd by her heart-frozen cold ;
But that I burn much more in boiling sweat,
And feel my flames augmented manifold ?
What more miraculous thing may be told,
That fire, which all things melts, should harden ice ;
And ice which is congeal'd with senseless cold,
Should kindle fire by wonderful device ?
Such is the power of love in gentle mind
That it can alter all the course of kind.

We submit that these two poems are without the smallest interdependence, and that the thought or content of the one does not arise out of the thought or content of the other, though broadly both deal with facets of the same subject. Read as we have printed them, they do not in the least appear to be out of sequence ; yet as a fact the second sonnet is No. 30 in the Spenser sequence, and the first No. 31. It must not be supposed that this complete separability and independence is always so clear as in the example we have given ; but it obtains far more generally than would appear to be supposed by the sticklers for sequence development ; and we are inclined to emphasise it not only as further proof of our theory that the sonnet is the preordained form for the complete expression of a certain special kind of poetical emotion, but as tending also to prove that

THE ENGLISH SONNET

sonnet-sequence which shall be a sequence in the deep sense of sequence—as, for instance, in the chapters of a novel, the stages of an argument, the stanzas of a poem like *St. Agnes' Eve*, or the verses of a ballad—is next door to an impossibility. In any case, for the modern sonnet, the sequence is in our opinion an improfitable and even destructive device. Do as he will, and strive as he may, the poet of the modern sonnet sequence is driven sooner or later into the negation of the first and prime principle of sonnet organisation which is that the octet should be an " onset " or " opening " and cannot in the nature of things properly take the form of a " climax " or " closing." To his article on the sonnet in *Sonnets of the Nineteenth Century*, Sharp prefixes a sequence of two sonnets addressed to Dante Gabriel Rossetti. The octet of the second of these commences thus :—

> Yet even if Death indeed with pitiful sign
> Bade us drink deep of some oblivious draught,
> Is it not well to know, ere we have quaffed
> The soul-deceiving poppied anodyne,
> That not in vain erewhile we drank the wine
> Of life?

We say that " yet even if Death " is palpably the beginning of a sestet and not of an octet at all. It is so to the ear and so to the intellect,

SEQUENCE

and it controverts in two ways the author's own rule that a sonnet must be absolutely complete in itself, i.e. it must be the evolution of *one* thought, or *one* emotion, or *one* poetically apprehended fact; for, firstly, it is dependent on some thought or emotion which has gone before it, and therefore possesses only that kind of completeness which belongs prescriptively to the sestet, and, secondly, it avows by implication that the sestet of the sonnet which precedes it has not been brought to its full conclusion, and is therefore incomplete. When poets of the calibre of George Meredith and Dr. Bridges turn their hands to the sonnet sequence, they come by necessity to pretty much the same ends. That is to say, they succeed in writing single sonnets of great beauty only when sequentiality is dropped, and sonnets which are fundamentally irregular and therefore jarring and tiresome, when sequence is maintained. Sonnet sequences exhibit the further disadvantage of an *embarras de richesses*. The finer, the more exquisite, and the more sustained their beauty, the more difficult are they to get through. Course after course of the same bird served with the same delicate sauce and on the same golden dish wearies even the most redoubtable gourmet. The average sonnet sequence is really a sonnet

THE ENGLISH SONNET

surfeit. To be read and enjoyed and to have their true force as poetry, all the great sonnet sequences, no matter whose, have to be "dipped into." No living man will ever convince us that he read through the sonnets of Shakespeare from No. 1 to No. 144 at a sitting and for pleasure. And we should like to wager that no man living or dead ever did it twice. This is not to decry the sonnet; but simply to say that the faculty for the sustained appreciation of beauty is limited. Practically every one of the great sonnets to be found in the sequences, whether early or modern, reads more finely and moves more powerfully out of its alleged (or real) context than in it. Five hundred people know almost off by heart half a dozen or so of Shakespeare's sonnets, for one who possesses, or ever will possess, more than a nodding acquaintance with them all. And for one person who reads Drayton sequentially, probably a thousand keep the *Love-Parting* for remembrance like so much rosemary. Of course it may be argued that a hundred and forty-four unrelated sonnets of transcendent beauty by one hand would be just as trying and as wearing as a sequence. But we do not agree that this is so. Unfortunately literature is as yet unable to furnish us with a test. The nearest we can get to such a test is the sonnet

SEQUENCE

anthology, and we venture to suggest that any of them is more enthralling reading than any sequence. Broadly, therefore, we shall pronounce the sonnet sequence, considered as a complete work of itself, to be technically vicious and undesirable. In the modern sonnet, at any rate, its tendency is to induce violations of the sonnet law which are distressing and ought not to be tolerated. The poet who writes two sonnets in sequence is tacitly admitting that his first flight has failed, and that his emotion or passion or idea has not been brought to its proper focus. He will say that, on the contrary, his subject has so moved and uplifted him that he overflows, and produces two sonnets instead of one. To which our reply is that he has not really written two sonnets, but a poem in two fourteen-line stanzas, which, inasmuch as the stanzas are of a form which peculiarly suggest the sonnet, fail not only as sonnets, but as stanzas. This is not an arbitrary judgment, but will be found to have its justification in poetic and in formal and melodic law. The whole of the finest sonnets in the language are separate and complete poems and not dependent upon precedent poems. If Milton had set himself about it, he could easily have added another

THE ENGLISH SONNET

sonnet to the sonnet on his blindness; it is to be presumed that Wordsworth could just have readily composed two sonnets on Westminster Bridge as he composed one ; and had he been so minded, Keats could have written at least six sonnets about the Elgin marbles. But each of them was a great poet and a great sonneteer, and the great sonneteer knows that once at heaven's gate he must be content with a moment's sojourn—that the same bloom is not perfected twice, that the same lightning flash will not recur for all eternity. We are not forgetting the exceptions which might be cited against us, particularly in the cases of Keats and Wordsworth. There are three sonnets of Keats appearing under the general title of "Woman, when I behold thee," and concerned with one train of thought. The first of these, however, is complete and brought to a full conclusion of itself, and the same holds true of the second. The third also has essential completeness, although the first line of it bears undoubted reference to the precedent sestet :—

> Ah ! who can e'er forget so fair a being ?
> Who can forget her half-retiring sweets ?
> God ! she is like a milk-white lamb that bleats
> For man's protection. Surely the All-seeing,

THE SESTET-OCTET

Who joys to see us with his gifts agreeing,
Will never give him pinions, who entreats
Such innocence to ruin—who vilely cheats
A dove-like bosom. In truth there is no freeing

One's thoughts from such a beauty ; when I hear
A lay that once I saw her hand awake,
Her form seems floating palpable, and near ;
Had I e'er seen her from an arbour take
A dewy flower, oft would that hand appear,
And o'er my eyes the trembling moisture shake.

" Ah ! who can e'er forget so fair a being " is a proper octet-opening. The mind does not demand that anything antecedent should have been expressed, and is quite content to accept the line for an onset or opening. As a fact, however, something antecedent has been expressed. The antecedent sestet concludes : —

And when I mark
Such charms with mild intelligences shine,
My ear is open like a greedy shark,
To catch the tunings of a voice divine.

Therefore, " so fair a being " is intended sequentially. But if we accept it sequentially —as in the circumstances we are bound to do—the line at once becomes a sestet line ; and the poem loses its constructional and emotional symmetry. So that here we have an instance of the transformation by sequence, of a more or less passable sonnet into a

THE ENGLISH SONNET

fourteen-line poem, which is not a sonnet. Read by themselves the fourteen lines are a sonnet, though defiant of the rule as to the pause, and weakened by double rhymes; in sequence they cease to be a sonnet because they fail in the grand principle of the sonnet, which is a poem form to itself and not a mere stanza. The instances of sequence in Wordsworth are frequent. As a clear case of sequential intention the three " sonnets " entitled *The Widow on Windermere Side* might be interesting if they were a trifle better poetry. But nobody can read them with the feeling that they are sonnets, and though in the third the poet struggles valiantly for a convincing sestet effect, with a view doubtless to compensating us for the general dreariness of the work, he does not achieve. In the *River Duddon* and *Punishment of Death* series the sequence *qua* sequence cannot be said to shine any the more brightly. Indeed, with the rarest exceptions the sonnet here becomes a veritable " glow-worm lamp " for the cheering of mild Wordsworth and nobody else. The *Ecclesiastical Sketches* and the *Sonnets Dedicated to Liberty* cannot be claimed for sequences. The *Sketches* offer six or seven examples of two sonnets on the same subject, or two sonnets of which the second is professedly a continuation

SUBJECT-MATTER

of the first; though there is no real linking-up or interdependence; and while the *Liberty* sonnets include examples of actual and undeniable sequence, the finest part of the collection will be found to consist of single and independent pieces, which are just as great and just as moving whether printed separately or together.

Next arises the incidental question of sonnet subject-matter. We have already made some reference to this in our summary of the sonnet legislation. It is essential that a sonnet should have in it something more than the poetry to be obtained out of description, relation, fancy, verbal felicity or chiming melody—something which, in Wordsworth's words,

> Comes not by casting in a formal mould,
> But from its own divine vitality.

To define the precise nature and limits of the subject of that something were idle and supererogatory. The supreme poet might conceivably write a fine sonnet on the multiplication table, or the law of torts, or petroleum emulsion, or hematogeneous infiltrations of the kidney. One of the least successful sonnets ever written is the handiwork of a supreme poet, who, legitimately enough, entitled it *Steamboats, Via-*

THE ENGLISH SONNET

ducts and Railways, and one of the most tremendous sonnets ever written has for its subject, "lust in action." There is nothing in "steamboats, viaducts and railways" as a subject, which precludes the great sonnet; while as for "lust in action" as a subject there might seem to be everything that is calculated to daunt the most aspiring. Wordsworth's locomotory sonnet fails, not because of its subject and not even out of an unpoetical conception of the subject, but simply for want of poetical grip; and Shakespeare's quasi-physiological sonnet succeeds despite the obscure poetic quality of its subject, because the subject is conceived and exploited in the light of high poetic genius. Clearly, therefore, we must attempt no definite or absolute rule of sonnet-subject. The early sonneteers appear to have been of a mind that the true and almost exclusive subject of sonnet content is the passion of love. They wrote, not ballads, but sonnets to their mistresses' eyebrows; and for purposes outside the presentation and discussion of the grand passion they had little or no use for the sonnet. Any impulse devoid of what the fictionists call "a love interest" was not regarded as an impulse to sonnet writing. It was not till Milton that Cupid and Venus lost the sole empery of

JONES!

the sonnet kingdom, and it was not till Wordsworth that it was fully discovered to us for a kingdom wherein the poet might traffic not only for love and the gauds and trappings of love, but for weightier, more various, and more shining merchandise. Though in all, perhaps, Wordsworth wrote no greater number of supreme sonnets than Milton, he nevertheless turned out something like four hundred pieces in the sonnet form as against Milton's twenty-three. He showed us indeed that the subjects for the sonnet are as numberless and infinite as the subjects for poetry at large, and limited only by the bounds of human observation, human emotion, and human imagination. A poet who had to look for his sonnet sanctions to the lofty austerities of Milton, and the resplendencies and " sugar'd " passions or fancies of Milton's predecessors, and could still solemnly pen a " sonnet," beginning

Jones! While from Calais, southward you and I

might be considered to have possessed not only the courage of a peculiar and dangerous conviction, but contempt for a noble tradition. Yet it was this very disposition and eagerness to look down as it were, to see in " the meanest flower that blows,"

Thoughts that do often lie too deep for tears,

THE ENGLISH SONNET

that gave to Wordsworth what we may call his infinite sonnet variety and helped us to our modern understanding of the English sonnet as a poetic instrument of practically unrestricted range. At the same time we must not shut our eyes to the fact that the subject-matter of the sonnet has its degrees of suitability, just as there are degrees of suitability in the subject-matter for other forms of poetry. Broadly, of course, the more intrinsically poetical the theme, the finer may we expect the sonnet to be. The most exalted theme can be mishandled, though the chances are that a sonneteer of authentic impulse and parts will not mishandle it. And equally, the least promising theme may sometimes be lifted almost to the pinnacles. So that the selective power arises within and not without, and we are faced with the truism that any subject upon which a fine sonnet has been written was a fine subject for a sonnet. The impulse must always be the ultimate and deciding influence. We can recall few sonnet failures which are directly attributable to a defect of subject, and this applies to the dullest and most pedestrian of the moderns, including Wordsworth at his dullest and most pedestrian. Let us look a little closely into the classic case of the aforementioned " Jones ! "

ONE OF THE WORST

> Jones ! While from Calais, southward you and I
> Urged our accordant steps, this public way
> Streamed with the pomp of a too-credulous day,
> When faith was pledged to new-born liberty :
> A homeless sound of joy was in the sky ;
> The antiquated earth, as one might say,
> Beat like the heart of man : songs, garlands, play,
> Banners and happy faces far and nigh !
> And now, sole register that these things were,
> Two solitary greetings have I heard,
> " Good morrow, citizen ! " a hollow word
> As if a dead man spake it ! yet despair
> Touches me not, though pensive as a bird
> Whose vernal coverts winter hath laid bare.

Now what is wrong here ? It seems that on an occasion when Jones—we had almost said " damn him ! "—and the poet of these fourteen lines " urged their accordant steps " southward from Calais, they did so in the midst of public rejoicing. The people were celebrating " a too-credulous day when faith was pledged to new-born liberty " ; the day in question being July 14th, 1790, upon which, as Wordsworth explains in a footnote, Louis XVI " took the oath of fidelity to the new constitution." There was " a sound of joy in the *sky* " and " banners and happy faces far and nigh." On August 7, 1802, our sonneteer travels the same road, this time unaccompanied by the egregious Jones ; but possessed of the knowledge that the new-

THE ENGLISH SONNET

born liberty of the people has been short-lived. Cheerfulness no longer sings in the air, as it were. There are no more happy faces. Twice the solitary traveller hears the "Good morrow, citizen!" which had formerly been the salutation of the freed, but it is given in a hollow half-hearted way, " as if a dead man spake it." Naturally the poet is filled with brooding regrets; yet his faith in the ultimate triumph of liberty is such that he refuses to despair.

It cannot be disputed that out of these circumstances and the reflections they induce a considerable sonnet might have been put together. The subject is sufficiently lofty, inasmuch as it relates to liberty and the happiness of mankind. It offers the meditative and emotional opportunities necessary to poetry, and proper scope for the play of the imagination. As a subject, the intellect discovers no fault in it. Why then does the sonnet come to grief? In the first place, of course, we have "Jones!" which is, to say the least, disconcerting, and, really, settles the hash of the poem right off. Before we recover our breath, we get the capital "I" for a rhyme sound and we know that we are in for a more or less feebly rhymed octet. Then we have the periphrastic "urged our

THE GIN-MULE

accordant steps," and at the end of the line a second hackneyed rhyme sound, " way." Almost immediately following comes

> A homeless sound of joy was *in the sky,*

and

> The antiquated earth, *as one might say;*

Of course, as a fact, the " sound " was in the air and not in " the sky." Even " Jones," whoever he may have been, would have boggled at a sound in the sky. But "sky" is an old, unhappy, spavined, gin-mule rhyme for " I " and " liberty," and consequently " sky " had to serve. Then ponder on " as one might say," in any poem, much less a sonnet; and figuring here for no reason in the world except feebly to eke out an already feeble rhyme scheme. " Play " in the next line is another easy eking out, if not quite so flagrant; while to describe " good morrow, citizen!" (in line 11) as " a hollow word " is grossly to misemploy the substantive " word " whether in its singular or collective meaning. One may say " a word in your ear," and follow it with twenty words; and one may say " this is my word to you," and follow it with a discourse; but " a hollow word " as descriptive of " good morrow, citi-

THE ENGLISH SONNET

zen!" is bad idiom and worse poetry. There is a certain confusion, also, in such phrases as "a too-credulous day," and "pensive as a bird whose vernal covers winter hath *laid bare*"; and though both of them may be upheld, they nevertheless jar on the mind of the reader. Thus we perceive that a sonnet of fine subject, and proper organisation (for the octet and sestet systems are both fundamentally sound) and containing such good poetry as

> The antiquated earth
> Beat like the heart of man,

and

> . A hollow word,
> As if a dead man spake it,

is utterly spoiled and made waste by blemishes so obvious that the pointing of them out were work for the schoolmaster, rather than the critic. We will never believe that Wordsworth "knew no better," or that he sinned out of carelessness. His sin was the besetting sin of nearly all sonneteers, namely, downright indolence.

There is a further aspect of the question of sonnet-subject, which is this. Certain themes, while in themselves desirable and legitimate, have already been so perfectly or

THE THING ACCOMPLISHED

exhaustively dealt with in sonnet poetry that it is doubtful whether they ought ever again to be attempted. To take an extreme instance, no poet of parts would dream of committing himself to a sonnet on the precise subject of Keats's masterpiece about Chapman's Homer. Even though the impulse and inspiration which fired Keats were to be reproduced in the breast of another sonnet poet new lighted upon Chapman, we should hold it incumbent upon that poet to refrain. And he should refrain, not so much out of a fear to challenge comparisons, as out of respect for what has been supremely well done. We think that this principle of abstention should apply also in regard to less particular subjects. Sonnets which by their subject or thought, or even by their mood, recall too insistently the approved work of powerful pens, should not be written. We are not now referring to the mere copy or imitation, which usually carries its condemnation on the face of it; but to the much more frequent effusion wherein a fine conception or emotional explication is duplicated. The modern offenders in this article are numerous, and some of them eminent. One cannot quite accuse them of the airing of borrowed feathers, but they would seem to suffer from an over-

THE ENGLISH SONNET

weening desire to screen the "wasteful glitterings" of more opulent birds with their own spread tails. The modern sonnet should be a proud and independent poem; a lighting up of new beauty and new phases of thought, rather than a going back for the re-painting of the old. There should be honour among sonneteers, a recognition that what may pass prettily for "meum," is not uncommonly three parts "tuum."

Lastly, and very briefly, we may deal with what is known as "manner." There are poets who pride themselves on producing sonnets "in the manner of Shakespeare," or "the manner of Milton" or "the manner of Rossetti." "Mannered" poems of other forms are not considered admirable, and run the risk of being frowned down for "echoes," or "such-and-such-a-poet and water." But the "mannered" sonnet sometimes obtains great vogue and applause. In our opinion it should be avoided. We are inclined to the view that the nearer we get to pure poetry the less surely are we able to recognise the authorship of that poetry by intuition. This is probably against all the doctrine. We are told that the sure mark of a great poet is that he has a "cry" or "inflection" or "accent" of his own; perhaps this is true. On the

MANNER

other hand, we think that the sure mark of great poetry is that it might have been written by almost any great poet.

>Queens have died young and fair.
>. . . . .
>There is a budding morrow in midnight.
>. . . . .
>All pains the immortal spirit must endure.
>. . . . .
>Whose dwelling is the light of setting suns.
>. . . . .
>Extort her crimson secret from the rose.
>. . . . .
>The inheritors of unfulfilled renown
>Far in the unapparent.
>. . . . .
>And looks commercing with the skies.
>. . . . .
>On that best portion of a good man's life,
>His little, nameless, unremembered acts
>Of kindness and of love.
>. . . . .
>Her gentle limbs she did undress
>And lay down in her loveliness.
>. . . . .
>And even the weariest river
>Winds somewhere safe to sea.
>. . . . .
>Now folds the lily all her sweetness up.
>. . . . .
>White as the hand of Moses blows the thorn.
>. . . . .

THE ENGLISH SONNET

And beauty crept into a rose.

. . . . .

Holding in vain each other close.

. . . . .

And thou shalt envy me my shadowy crag
And softly feeding vulture.

These, and the thousand things like them which haunt the memory, are of the very essence of poetry—and really what we mean by poetry. Yet for any " manner " they have about them, they might all have been written by one and the same poet. We conclude, therefore, that poised at his highest the poet gets rid of accent, and that the purest poetical speech is a " cry " to itself. In a sonnet a poet should be twice poised at his highest, and the brevity of the form calls for the purest poetical speech, leaving no room for anything unexalted. Consequently we submit that " mannered " sonnets are defective sonnets; even when, as is rarely the case, the manner is the poets own. Properly speaking, only Shakespeare and Milton have sonnet manners of their own. To his contemporaries, perhaps, Shakespeare did not seem mannered in the least, but wrote in the best poetical language of his period; which, making allowances for the minor effects of time—is still the best poetical language. Milton, on the other hand,

MANNER

did arrive at a tremendous manner, yet the actual poetry in him is unmannered. Whatever may be the value of manner in either of them, however, such a value does not exist for the modern sonnet.

BOOK TWO
THE SONNETEERS

SIR THOMAS WYATT
1503-1542

HENRY HOWARD, EARL OF SURREY
1516-1547

MINOR ELIZABETHAN SONNET CYCLES

THE first sonnets in English are to be found in *Tottel's Miscellany* or *Book of Songs and Sonettes*, which was published in 1557. The volume consists mainly of the poetical writings of Sir Thomas Wyatt and Henry Howard, Earl of Surrey, who, with Chaucer, may be considered to have laid the technical foundations of modern English poetry. Besides being a poet, Wyatt was a scholar and a courtier. He has been described as "one of the most accomplished men of his day . . . dextrous and subtle in the management of affairs yet of spotless honour and integrity." Surrey, for his part, though equally accomplished, and a distinguished soldier, lay some time in the Fleet prison "for challenging a gentleman," and later was committed "for roystering and breaking windows in the streets at night." So that the sonnet began well. Both Wyatt and

THE ENGLISH SONNET

Surrey had resided in Italy, both were admirers of Petrarc and the Italianate literature, and conjointly they transplanted the sonnet form into the poetic of their own country. The credit of having written the first English sonnet is ascribed by some authorities to Wyatt and by others to Surrey. We are inclined to agree with Leigh Hunt that Wyatt probably wrote the first English poem constructed on the Petrarcan principle. It is a fairly crude piece of work, and we reproduce it because of its formal interest rather than its poetical value. We have Bowdlerized it to the extent of altering one word:

> Cesar, when that the traytor of Egipt,
> With thonorable hed did him present,
> Covering his gladnesse, did represent
> Playnt with his teres onteward, as it is writt;
> And Hannyball, eke, when fortune him [spit]
> Clene from his reign, and from all his intent
> Laught to his folke, whom sorrowe did torment,
> His cruel dispite for to dis-gorge and quit.
> So chaunceth it oft, that every passion
> The mind hideth, by color contrary,
> With fayned visage now sad, now mery:
> Whereby if I laught, any time or season,
> It is: for bicause I have nother way
> To cloke my care, but under sport and play.

It is to be noted that Wyatt opens the ball with a proper Petrarcan octet followed by a sinful

WYATT AND SURREY

close rhyme and rhymed couplet. In other respects the sonnet rule is observed. A better sonnet of Wyatt's, both as poetry and technically, is the following :

> The longe love, that in my thought I harber
> And in my heart doth keep his residence,
> Into my face preaseth with bold pretence,
> And therein campeth, spreding his banner.
> She that me learneth to love and to suffer,
> And willes that my trust, and lustes negligence
> Be reined by reason, shame and reverence,
> With his hardinesse taketh displeasure.
> Where with all unto the heart's forest he fleeth,
> Leaving his enterprise with paine and crye,
> And there him hideth and not appeareth,
> What may I do when my master feareth,
> But in the field with him to live and die?
> For good is the life, ending faithfully.

Here again we have the proper sonnet structure, and the due observance of the volta or turn, but the sestet concludes with *two* rhymed couplets.

The sonnets of Surrey are much more competent, and incomparably finer in the poetical sense. Here, however, great liberties are taken with the Petrarcan scheme, and while in some cases a pretty poem results, it has no claim to consideration as a sonnet except in respect of the number of its lines. The example we quote is the familiar *Description of Spring, wherin each thing renews save only the Lover :*

THE ENGLISH SONNET

The soote season, that bud and bloom forth brings,
With green hath clad the hill, and eke the vale;
The nightingale with feathers new she sings;
The turtle to her mate hath told her tale.
Summer is come, for every spray now springs;
The hart hath hung his old head on the pale;
The buck in brake his winter coat he flings;
The fishes flete with new repaired scale;
The adder all her slough away she flings;
The swift swallow pursueth the flies smale;
The busy bee her honey now she mings;
Winter is worn that was the flowers' bale.
And thus I see, among these pleasant things,
Each care decays, and yet my sorrow springs!

This sonnet is rhymed throughout on two sounds, and the sweetness of the melodic result cannot be gainsaid. But it is obvious that a number of pieces so rhymed would be cloying to the ear.

Tottell's Miscellany had a great vogue and went through seven editions between 1557 and 1584. It started a new fashion in English poetry and gave an entirely new turn to poetical craftmanship. Following the later editions came a steady stream of sonnet cycles or sequences including those of Sidney, Spenser, and Shakespeare, and various lesser performers whom we may notice briefly. In 1581 was published the Ἑκατομπαθια, *or Passionate Century of Love,* by Thomas Watson, whom Steevens pronounced to be a more elegant sonneteer

THOMAS WATSON

than Shakespeare. The appended effusion of Watson, from a later work, *The Teares of Fancie*, provides a sufficient commentary on Steevens's judgment. It is as good as anything Watson wrote, and as full of "teares." Except for the fact that it is on the pure English model, we fail to see how it can be compared with Shakespeare at all.

> I saw the object of my pining thought,
> Within a garden of sweet nature's placing:
> Where is an arbour artificial wrought,
> By workman's wondrous skill the garden gracing
> Did boast his glory, glory far renowned,
> For on his shady boughs my mistress slept,
> And with a garland of his branches crowned,
> Her dainty forehead from the sun ykept.
> Imperious love upon her eyelids tending,
> Playing his wanton sports at every beck,
> And into every finest limb descending,
> From eyes to lips, from lips to ivory neck:
> And every limb supplied and 't every part,
> Had free access, but durst not touch her heart.

The whole of the sonnets in the *Passionate Century* are eighteen lines in length. Each of them is really a translation of some other author, and preceded by an ingenuous admission of the source from which it is borrowed. Strictly, of course, the verses are not sonnets.

A year after the publication of *Astrophel and Stella*, that is to say, in 1591, Samuel Daniel

THE ENGLISH SONNET

issued his famous *Delia,* a sonnet sequence of fifty-four pieces, of which we reproduce two:

> Fair is my love, and cruel as she's fair;
> Her brow shades frown, altho' her eyes are sunny;
> Her smiles are lightning, though her pride despair;
> And her disdains are gall, her favours honey.
> A modest maid, deck'd with a blush of honour,
> Whose feet do tread green paths of youth and love;
> The wonder of all eyes that look upon her:
> Sacred on earth; design'd a saint above;
> Chastity and Beauty, which are deadly foes,
> Live reconciled friends within her brow;
> And had she Pity to conjoin with those,
> Then who had heard the plaints I utter now?
> For had she not been fair, and thus unkind,
> My muse had slept, and none had known my mind.

> I must not grieve, my love, whose eyes would read
> Lines of delight, whereon her youth might smile;
> Flowers have time before they come to seed,
> And she is young, and now must sport the while.
> And sport, sweet maid, in season of these years,
> And learn to gather flowers before they wither;
> And where the sweetest blossom first appears,
> Let love and youth conduct thy pleasures thither,
> Lighten forth smiles to clear the clouded air,
> And calm the tempest which my sighs do raise:
> Pity and smiles do best become the fair;
> Pity and smiles must only yield thee praise.
> Make me to say, when all my griefs are gone,
> Happy the heart that sigh'd for such a one.

The octet of the first of the foregoing is in rhymed couplets as regards the six opening

DANIEL AND LODGE

lines; but the sestet is on a sound Petrarcan model. The second sonnet is on the pure English model with the pause in the proper place.

In 1593 Thomas Lodge published *Phillis Honoured with Pastoral Sonnets* and Giles Fletcher his *Licia, or Poems of Love in Honour of the admirable and singular virtues of his Lady*. Neither of these works contains anything specially notable; though both were admired in their day. In 1594 appeared the *Diana* of Henry Constable, who, though of no great parts as a poet, doubtless helped to settle the true form of the English sonnet pure and simple. We append a sample of Constable's work, which, as will be seen, is rhymed on the Shakespearean scheme, but is without the octet pause:

> To live in hell, and heaven to behold,
> To welcome life, and die a living death,
> To sweat with heat, and yet be freezing cold,
> To grasp at stars, and lie the earth beneath,
> To tread a maze that never shall have end,
> To burn in sighs, and starve in daily tears,
> To clime a hill, and never to descend,
> Giants to kill, and quake at childish fears,
> To pine for food, and watch th' Hesperian tree,
> To thirst for drink, and nectar still to draw,
> To live accurst, whom men hold blest to be,
> And weep those wrongs, which never creature saw :
> If this be love, if love in these be founded,
> My heart is love, for these in it are grounded.

THE ENGLISH SONNET

This, of course, is pure rhetoric, and similar in thought to sundry better-known pieces by other hands. In the same year appeared *Sonnets To The Fairest Celia*, by W. Percy, who observes the turn but, like Constable, is addicted to the double rhyme and frequently uses it for the clinch :

> Receive these writs, my sweet and dearest friend,
> The lively patterns of my lifeless body ;
> Where thou shalt find in ebon pictures penn'd,
> How I was meek, but thou extremely bloody.
> I'll walk forlorn along the willow shades,
> Alone, complaining of a ruthless dame ;
> Where'er I pass, the rocks, the hills, the glades,
> In piteous yells shall sound her cruel name.
> There I will wail the lot which fortune sent me,
> And make my moans unto the savage ears ;
> The remnant of the days which Nature lent me,
> I'll spend them all, conceal'd, in ceaseless tears.
> Since unkind fates permit me not t' enjoy her,
> No more (burst eyes !) I mean for to annoy her.

The remaining sonnet cycles of importance in this period are Barnaby Barnes's *Divine Centurie of Spiritual Sonnets* (1595), Richard Barnefield's *Cynthia* (1595), William Smith's *Chloris* (1596), *Diella*, by R. L., gentleman (1596), *Fidessa*, by R. Griffen (1596), *Aurora*, by William Alexander, Earl of Sterline (1604), and the *Sonnets* of Joshua Sylvester (1610). From the *Divine Centurie of Spiritual Sonnets* we take the following :

THE DIVINE CENTURIE

Unto my spirit lend an angel's wing
By which it might mount to that place of rest
Where seraphs in their joy for ever sing
(Each with his love, each with his heavenly mate)
And know not agony of mind or breast,
For I in bitterness with death have strove,
And, wandering here and there all desolate,
Seek with my plaints to match that mournful dove.
No joy of ought that under heaven doth hove,
Can comfort me but her own joyous sight:
Whose sweet aspect both God and man can move
In her unspotted pleasance to delight.
Dark is my day whiles her fair light I miss
And dead my life that waits such lively bliss.

Barnefielde wrote several really fine pieces which, however, are not suitable for quotation. The lines appended may serve to show him at his technical average:

It is reported of fair Thetis' son
Achilles, famous for his chivalry,
His noble mind, and magnanimity,
That when the Trojan wars were new begun,
Whos'ever was deep-wounded with his spear,
Could never be re-cured of his maim,
Nor ever after be made whole again,
Except with that spear's rust he holpen were:
Even so it fareth with my fortune now,
Who being wounded with her piercing eye,
Must either thereby find a remedy,
Or else to be reliev'd I know not how.
Then, if thou hast a mind still to annoy me,
Kill me with kisses, if thou wilt destroy me.

THE ENGLISH SONNET

The *Chloris* of William Smith includes the following conventional protest against the conventional sonnet thought of the time :

> My love, I cannot thy rare beauties place
> Under those forms which many writers use.
> Some like to stones compare their mistress' face
> Some in the name of flowers do love abuse ;
> Some make their love a goldsmith's shop to be,
> Where orient pearls and precious stones abound :
> In my conceit these far do disagree,
> The perfect praise of beauty forth to sound.
> O Chloris, thou dost imitate thyself !
> Self-imitating, passeth precious stones ;
> For all the Eastern-India golden pelf,
> Thy red and white with purest fair attones,
> Matchless for beauty Nature hath thee fram'd
> Only unkind and cruel thou art nam'd.

R. L.—" gentleman "—produced some of the most workmanlike sonnets of the Elizabethan period. On the whole, however, they are stronger in diction than in passion or feeling :

> When Love had first besieg'd my heart's strong wall,
> Rampir'd and countermur'd with chastity,
> And had with ordnance made his tops to fall,
> Stooping their glory to his surquedry ;
> I call'd a parley, and withal did crave
> Some composition, or some friendly peace :
> To this request he his consent soon gave,
> As seeming glad such cruel wars should cease.

SLEEP

I, nought mistrusting, open'd all the gates,
Yea, lodg'd him in the palace of my heart;
When lo! in dead of night he seeks his mates,
And shows each traitor how to play his part;
With that they fir'd my heart, and thence 'gan fly,
Their names, sweet smiles, fair face, and piercing eye.

Griffen's best sonnet is on the subject of Sleep, and may be compared with sundry other effusions on the same theme, including that of Daniel, by which it appears to have been inspired:

Care-charmer sleep, sweet ease in misery,
The captive's liberty, and his freedom's song,
Balm of the bruised heart, man's chief felicity,
Brother of quiet death, when life is too too long;
A comedy it is, and now an history,
What is not sleep unto the tired mind?
It easeth him that toils, and him that's sorry,
It makes the deaf to hear, to see the blind.
Ungentle sleep, thou helpest all but me,
For, when I sleep, my soul is vexed most:
It is Fidessa that doth master thee,
If she approach, alas, thy power is lost!
But here she is—see, how he runs amain;
I fear at night he will not come again.

Daniel's sonnet on Sleep runs as follows:

Care-charmer Sleep, son of the sable Night,
Brother to Death, in silent darkness born,
Relieve my anguish, and restore the light;
With dark forgetting of my care return,

THE ENGLISH SONNET

>And let the day be time enough to mourn
>The shipwreck of my ill-adventured youth ;
>Let waking eyes suffice to wail their scorn,
>Without the torment of the night's untruth.
>Cease dreams, the images of day-desires,
>To model forth the passions of the morrow ;
>Never let rising Sun approve you liars
>To add more grief to aggravate my sorrow :
>Still let me sleep, embracing clouds in vain,
>And never wake to feel the day's disdain.

It is evident that Griffen stole from Daniel, and on the whole, perhaps, he did not steal to advantage.

Perhaps the best piece in Alexander's *Aurora* is Sonnet 10 :

>I swear, Aurora, by thy starry eyes,
>And by those golden locks whose lock none slips,
>And by the coral of thy rosy lips,
>And by the naked snows which beauty dyes ;
>I swear by all the jewels of thy mind,
>Whose like yet never worldly treasure bought,
>Thy solid judgment and thy generous thought,
>Which in this darken'd age have clearly shin'd ;
>I swear by those, and by my spotless love,
>And by my secret, yet most fervent fires,
>That I have never nurst but chaste desires
>And such as modesty might well approve.
>Then, since I love those virtuous parts in thee,
>Should'st thou not love this virtuous mind in me ?

Against the name of Joshua Sylvester we encounter in a biographical dictionary this

JOSHUA SYLVESTER

entry : " Achieved success neither as merchant nor poet." And yet Sylvester is the author of the following :

> Were I as base as is the lowly plain,
> And you, my Love, as high as heaven above,
> Yet should the thoughts of me your humble swain
> Ascend to heaven, in honour of my Love.
> Were I as high as heaven above the plain,
> And you, my Love, as humble and as low
> As are the deepest bottoms of the main,
> Where'er you were, with you my love should go.
> Were you the earth, dear Love, and I the skies,
> My love should shine on you like to the sun,
> And look upon you with ten thousand eyes
> Till heaven wax'd blind, and till the world were done.
> Where'er I am, below, or else above you,
> Where'er you are, my heart shall truly love you.

There is a simple honesty of emotion about that which, to our mind, is worth a wilderness of ornate protestation. What is more, the sonnet is admirably built, on the proper two-poem system; it has the correct pause and a very noble turn, and the concluding couplet or clinch is adequate and effective in spite of the double rhyme. Some of the lines in the octet and the whole of the sestet lines might easily have come out of a Shakespeare sonnet.

> Were I as high as heaven above the plain,
> And you, my Love, as humble and as low
> As are the deepest bottoms of the main,

THE ENGLISH SONNET

and

> Were you the earth, dear Love, and I the skies,
> My love should shine on you like to the sun,
> And look upon you with ten thousand eyes
> Till heaven wax'd blind, and till the world were done,

have the true sonnet breath and passion in them, and the piece as a whole must be placed among the best work of the period.

William Drummond of Hawthornden, "the friend of Drayton and Shakespeare" and quaintly described by Hunt as "the next best sonnet writer to Shakespeare *in point of time*," wrote a number of sonnets which are notable for their grave beauty and by reason of the fact that many of them turn on other subjects than the early sonneteer's stock subject of love. The following is an average specimen. Its sole fault lies in the irregularity of the octet rhyming:

> Of this fair volume which we World do name
> If we the sheets and leaves could turn with care,
> Of Him who it corrects, and did it frame,
> We clear might read the art and wisdom rare:
> Find out His power which wildest powers doth tame,
> His providence extending everywhere,
> His justice which proud rebels doth not spare,
> In every page, no period of the same.
> But silly we, like foolish children, rest
> Well pleased with colour'd vellum, leaves of gold,

CENTURIES AND CYCLES

> Fair dangling ribbands, leaving what is best,
> On the great Writer's sense ne'er taking hold;
> Or if by chance we stay our minds on aught,
> It is some picture on the margin wrought.

In discussing generally these early sonneteers, we must note that if their performance is not tremendous as poetry, it nevertheless served a deep and high purpose in the development of poetic as well as in the development of the sonnet. The " centuries " and cycles which only the curious now read achieved great popularity in their day and generation, and helped to create in England an atmosphere of poetry and an emulation among poets, of which the best production of the Elizabethan age is the direct result. Without Wyatt and Surrey and their following we might not have had *The Faerie Queen* and Shakespeare's *Plays*, just as we most certainly should not have had Shakespeare's *Sonnets* and the sonnets of Sidney, Spenser, and Drayton. In our own time, perhaps, it is the greater poets who have made the lesser poets possible, but in the beginning it was the lesser poets who made possible the greater. This is especially so with regard to the vital matter of form. The Elizabethan giants had no imitators; being themselves imitators and superb improvers on the small men. Wyatt,

THE ENGLISH SONNET

Surrey, Daniel, Constable, Barnefielde and the rest of them did the spade work; Sidney, Drayton, Spenser, Marlowe, and Shakespeare built the edifices. For the scale and the line, we have to look to the former; for the music and the glory, we have to look to the latter.

SIR PHILIP SIDNEY

1554-1586

SIR PHILIP SIDNEY is the one English poet whose reputation may be said to depend entirely on his work as sonneteer. He wrote other poetry, but of itself it does not live; perhaps because, to a large extent, it consists of sonnet matter wasted in experimental moulds. The *Astrophel and Stella* collection of a hundred and ten pieces has always been taken to embody the best of Sidney, as indeed it does. But this fact has led to certain unfortunate misconceptions; the chief of them being that outside *Astrophel and Stella* he produced no sonnets of formal importance. Hence it happens that the rhyme-scheme of the *Stella* series, which to our thinking is ill-founded, has passed into a sort of authority; and is still one of the excuses of the apostles of irregularity. Sidney's scheme in the whole of the *Stella* sonnets is

OCTET: *a-b-b-a a-b-b-a;*
SESTET: *c-d-c-d-e-e* or *c-c-d-e-e-d.*

So that in this series we get a strict Petrarcan octet with either an irregular Petrarcan sestet,

THE ENGLISH SONNET

or a strict Shakespearean sestet; and never a complete sonnet on the Petrarcan scheme. The melodic effect is deplorable, and the sonnets necessarily lose by it. Elsewhere, however, and notably in the *Arcadia*, the poet rids himself of this bastardy, and it is then that we are brought to perceive that to judge him on *Astrophel and Stella* alone, as is the common tendency, means that we have overlooked some of his main claim to competence. We have printed " My true love hath my heart and I have his " on a separate page. But the *Arcadia* offers us a further fine example of the English sonnet pure and simple, which, if generally known, is not generally singled out as Sidney in his most accomplished attainment :

> Who doth desire that chaste his wife should be,
> First be he true, for truth doth truth deserve :
> Then such be he, as she his worth may see,
> And one man still credit with her preserve.
> Not toying kind, nor causelessly unkind,
> Not stirring thoughts, nor yet denying right,
> Not spying faults, nor in plain errors blind ;
> Never hard hand, nor ever reins too light.
> As far from want, as far from vain expense
> (The one doth force, the latter doth entice)
> Allow good company, but keep from thence
> All filthy mouths that glory in their vice :
> This done thou hast no more, but leave the rest
> To virtue, fortune, time, and woman's breast.

THE ENGLISH FORM

Quite apart from its subject, this sonnet has the balance and poise and restraint of the perfect piece of art. The appeal is to the intellect, but it is also to the spirit. The whole sonnet is admirably built and knit, and the emotional effect of the final couplet throws radiance over every word that has gone before. We lay special stress on the formal value of this piece and its more famous companion, because, together, they show that Sidney was no mere groper after the perfect English form, but actually achieved it, and produced at least one —if not two—examples of it which would not have disgraced the Shakespearean series itself.

Save on the ground of melodic defect resulting from failure to grasp the full significance of the Petrarcan rhyme-scheme on the one hand, or to recognise that a sestet on the pure English scheme demands an octet of alternately rhymed quatrains on four sounds, there is nothing in the *Astrophel and Stella* series which does not compel respect and applause. Perhaps of all the so-called "sequences," it is the most delicate and simply and sincerely human. Unlike his compeers, Sidney refrains from the painting of the lily and the gilding of refined gold. One is made to feel that this Stella of his is a woman, rare and radiant enough; uncertain, coy, and hard

THE ENGLISH SONNET

to please ; but neither a goddess nor a supercilious ravener of hearts. It is true that at times she appears to bring him pretty low. Sonnet 69 reads :

> Dear, why make you more of a dog than me ?
> If we do love, I burn, I burn in love ;
> If he wait well, I never thence would move ;
> If he be fair, yet but a dog can be ;
> Little he is, so little worth is he ;
> He barks, my songs thine own voice yet doth prove :
> Bidden, perhaps he fetchéd thee a glove,
> But I unbid, fetch even my soul to thee.
> Yet while I languish, him that bosom clips,
> That lap doth lap, nay lets, in spite of spite,
> This sour-breath'd mute taste of those sugar'd lips.
> Alas, if you grant only such delight
> To witless things, then Love, I hope—since wit
> Becomes a clog—will soon ease me of it.

But this and the like abjectness is not the lady's fault. Because the poet has seen her kiss her dog, he falls into conceits about it, and talks of " fetching his soul." Yet we know that the situation is not heart-shaking, and that the Comic and not the Tragic Muse is at work. On an occasion similarly taxing, Shakespeare and even Spenser would have been in dead earnest. Shakespeare might easily have written a line as to " tiger lips assoiled with currish breath," and Spenser might have ejaculated—

LOVES

> O saint that to the kennel dost descend
> With lips still to be kissed!

And both of them would have been right; for according to Shakespeare his love was the devil, and according to Spenser his love was a milk-white angel. But according to Sidney, his love was a woman. Printed apart from the *Stella* series there are four sonnets " made when his lady had pain in her face," in plain terms, one takes it, the toothache. In the absence of evidence to the contrary it seems probable that these sonnets were written as part of the *Stella* series:

> The scourge of life, and death's extreme disgrace
> The smoke of hell, the monster callèd Pain;
> Long shamed to be accurst in every place,
> By them who of his rude resort complain;
> Like crafty wretch, by time and travail taught,
> His ugly evil in other's good to hide
> Late harbours in her face, whom Nature wrought
> As treasure house where her best gifts do bide.
> And so by privilege of sacred seat—
> A seat where beauty shines and virtue reigns—
> He hopes for some small praise, since she hath great;
> Within her beams wrapping his cruel stains.
> Ah, saucy Pain! Let not thy error last;
> More loving eyes she draws, more hate thou hast.

The remaining three are just as well done, but, like the one quoted, they are on a different

THE ENGLISH SONNET

rhyme-scheme from the *Stella* sonnets proper, and this may account for their omission. Sonnet 101 of the series, beginning " Stella is sick," runs on almost the same lines of thought and conceit. This, however, is by the way. Our point is that the *Astrophel and Stella* sonnets are neither pompous nor tragic, nor written out of a too consistent desire to glorify or immortalise the subject of them, but simply by a flesh and blood poet of a flesh and blood woman, and that is why they have lasted side by side with the more ambitious outpourings of Shakespeare, and are far more generally read than the sonnets of Spenser. As to the much debated question of their " sincerity," all we need to know about them is that in the main they are apparently sincere poetry. One of the least emotional of them, Sonnet 15, is interesting both on account of its plain artificiality as love poetry, and because it epitomises a certain amount of sonnet history up to Sidney's time :

> You that do search for every purling spring
> Which from the ribs of old Parnassus flows,
> And every flower, not sweet perhaps, which grows
> Near thereabouts, into your poesie wring ;
> Yet that do dictionary's method bring
> Into your rhymes, running in rattling rows ;
> You that poor Petrarch's long deceasèd woes
> With new-born sighs and denizen'd wit do sing ;

ASTROPHEL AND STELLA

> You take wrong ways; these far-set helps be such
> As do bewray a want of inward touch,
> And sure at length stolen goods do come to light;
> But if, both for your love and skill, your name
> You seek to nurse at fullest breasts of Fame,
> Stella behold, and then begin to indite.

The man who wrote that took neither love nor art too seriously. But he knew all about the sonnet and the sonneteers of his time, and he had a greater respect for the sonnet than he had for the sonneteers. *Astrophel and Stella* was not published till five years after his death—that is to say, in 1591—and it has been argued, therefore, that either he set no great store by the work, or refrained from publication because " Stella " was Penelope Rich—another man's wife. We should think it quite as likely that he held them back for purposes of polish, or perhaps because he desired to add to them. In the original edition, the sequence comes to an abrupt end at Sonnet 108. Grosart incorporated the remaining two. Both are exceedingly fine, and the last of them, "Leave me, O Love," is of the pure English mould. But between 108 and 109 there is a pretty considerable jump of attitude, as it were. Up to 108 the poet has been a good deal of a poet for poetry's sake; inclined on the whole to hug and be well

THE ENGLISH SONNET

pleased with his alleged griefs so long as he could make music out of them. But in 109—the "Desire" sonnet—he breaks out even more fiercely than Shakespeare on the like matter. And for a finale in Sonnet 110 we get another blaze from a Sidney who has been hurt with something woundier than "the daily-vexing care," and is no longer in the humour to fetch his soul to a woman's feet in the manner of the little dog. It may well be that, if indeed these two sonnets were intended to round off the series, Sidney would wish to bridge the gulf between them and Sonnet 108 with pieces which would develop and lead up to the climax; and it may equally well be that he meditated an ending more in keeping with the general drift of the work. In any case it is evident that as it stands in the original edition the sequence is not complete, and that something was wanted to finish it. Sidney had no pronounced disposition to the fragment, and we think it reasonable to presume that he refrained from publishing because he was not ready. As far as it goes, *Astrophel and Stella* bears evidence of having been arranged and polished with the greatest care. There is not a slipshod or careless sonnet in the whole collection and scarcely a line that is halting or faulty; while if the sequentiality

POLISH

is of no particular account as a set unfolding in the story sense, it is altogether admirable in its avoidance of jar, too close repetition of sets of rhymes, monotony of mood, and so forth. Indeed, in these regards the series is a model of what such a series should be.

THE ENGLISH SONNET

No more, my dear, no more these counsels try;
O give my passions leave to run their race;
Let Fortune lay on me her worst disgrace;
Let folk o'ercharged with brain against me cry;
Let clouds bedim my face, break in mine eye;
Let me no steps but of lost labour trace;
Let all the earth with scorn recount my case,—
But do not will me from my love to fly.
I do not envy Aristotle's wit,
Nor do aspire to Cæsar's bleeding fame;
Nor ought do care though some above me sit;
Nor hope nor wish another course to frame,
But that which once may win thy cruel heart:
Thou art my wit, and thou my virtue art.

SIR PHILIP SIDNEY

Because I breathe not love to every one,
Nor do not use set colours for to wear,
Nor nourish special locks of vowèd hair,
Nor give each speech a full point of a groan,
The Courtly nymphs, acquainted with the moan
Of them which in their lips Love's standard bear:
What, he! (say they of me): now I dare swear
He cannot love; no, no, let him alone.
And think so still, so Stella know my mind;
Profess in deed I do not Cupid's art;
But you, fair maids, at length this true shall find,
That his right badge is but worn in the heart;
Dumb swans, not chattering pies, do lovers prove;
They love indeed who quake to say they love.

THE ENGLISH SONNET

Come, Sleep ! O Sleep, the certain knot of peace,
The baiting-place of wit, the balm of woe,
The poor man's wealth, the prisoner's release,
Th' indifferent judge between the high and low ;
With shield of proof shield me from out the prease
Of those fierce darts Despair at me doth throw :
O make me in those civil wars to cease ;
I will good tribute pay, if thou do so.
Take thou of me smooth pillows, sweetest bed,
A chamber deaf to noise and blind to light,
A rosy garland and a weary head :
And if these things, as being thine in right,
Move not thy heavy grace, thou shalt in me,
Livelier than elsewhere, Stella's image see.

SIR PHILIP SIDNEY

With how sad steps, O Moon, thou climb'st the skies,
How silently, and with how wan a face!
What, may it be that even in heav'nly place
That busy archer his sharp arrows tries?
Sure, if that long-with-love-acquainted eyes
Can judge of love, thou feel'st a lover's case,
I read it in thy looks; thy languisht grace,
To me, that feel the like, thy state descries.
Then, ev'n of fellowship, O Moon, tell me,
Is constant love deem'd there but want of wit?
Are beauties there as proud as here they be?
Do they above love to be lov'd, and yet
Those lovers scorn whom that love doth possess?
Do they call virtue there ungratefulness?

THE ENGLISH SONNET

Soul's joy, bend not those morning stars from me,
Where Virtue is made strong by Beauty's might ;
Where Love is chasteness, Pain doth learn delight,
And Humbleness grows one with Majesty.
Whatever may ensue, O let me be
Co-partner of the riches of that sight ;
Let not mine eyes be hell-driv'n from that light ;
O look, O shine, O let me die, and see.
For though I oft myself of them bemoan
That through my heart their beamy darts be gone,
Whose cureless wounds even now most freshly bleed,
Yet since my death-wound is already got,
Dear killer, spare not thy sweet-cruel shot ;
A kind of grace it is to slay with speed.

SIR PHILIP SIDNEY

Having this day my horse, my hand, my lance
Guided so well that I obtain'd the prize,
Both by the judgment of the English eyes
And of some sent from that sweet enemy France ;
Horsemen my skill in horsemanship advance,
Town-folks my strength ; a daintier judge applies
His praise to sleight which from good use doth rise ;
Some lucky wits impute it but to chance ;
Others, because of both sides I do take
My blood from them who did excel in this,
Think Nature me a man-at-arms did make.
How far they shot awry ! the true cause is,
Stella look'd on, and from her heav'nly face
Sent forth the beams which made so fair my race.

THE ENGLISH SONNET

Thou blind man's mark, thou fool's self-chosen snare,
Fond fancy's scum, and dregs of scattered thought,
Band of all evils ; cradle of causeless care ;
Thou web of will, whose end is never wrought :
Desire ! Desire ! I have too dearly bought
With price of mangled mind, thy worthless ware ;
Too long, too long, asleep thou hast me brought,
Who should'st my mind to higher things prepare.
But yet in vain thou hast my ruin sought ;
In vain thou mad'st me to vain things aspire ;
In vain thou kindlest all thy smoky fire ;
For Virtue hath this better lesson taught,—
Within myself to seek my only hire,
Desiring nought but how to kill Desire.

SIR PHILIP SIDNEY

Leave me, O Love, which reachest but to dust ;
And thou my mind, aspire to higher things ;
Grow rich in that which never taketh rust ;
Whatever fades, but fading pleasures brings,
Draw in thy beams, and humble all thy might
To that sweet yoke, where lasting freedoms be ;
Which breaks the clouds, and opens forth the light
That doth both shine and give us sight to see.
O take fast hold ; let that light be thy guide
In this small course which birth draws out to death,
And think how evil becometh him to slide,
Who seeketh heaven and comes of heav'nly breath,
Then farewell, world ; thy uttermost I see :
Eternal Love, maintain thy Life in me.

MICHAEL DRAYTON

1563–1631

THE position of Michael Drayton among the earlier sonneteers is very nearly paramount. His state may be accounted kingly. " Golden-mouthed Drayton " Guilpin calls him, and the epithet should stand ; for golden-mouthed he indisputably is. In some regards certain of his sonnets are greater even than Shakespeare's. They lack the sweetness and "proud pied April " pomp of the mightier poet, and they are seldom concerned with the deep and ultimate matters which are of the Shakespeare substance. But at times Drayton could climb, and at other times he exhibits qualities of poetic humour and irony which, in his sonnets, Shakespeare avoided. If the famous *Love-Parting* of Drayton had been a sonnet of the Shakespeare series it would have been recognised as one of the finest, if not indeed the finest, in the collection :—

> Since there's no help, come let us kiss and part ;
> Nay, I have done ; you get no more of me.

ONSETS

There is no onset in Shakespeare humanly to range with that. "When forty winters shall besiege thy brow, and dig deep trenches in thy beauty's field," "Shall I compare thee to a summer's day, Thou art more lovely and more temperate," "When in disgrace with fortune and men's eyes, I all alone beweep my outcast state," "Not marble, nor the gilded monuments of princes shall outlive this powerful rhyme," are tremendous enough; but they lack the emotion of the Drayton opening. Shakespeare begins like an emperor; Drayton like a man with a heart in his bosom. And nowhere has Shakespeare more than this tenderness of regret: —

> Shake hands for ever; cancel all our vows
> And when we meet at any time again
> Be it not seen in either of our brows
> That we one jot of former love retain.

And mark with what a true turn and sweep Drayton enters upon the sestet and how surely and nobly he develops it: —

> Now at the last gasp of Love's latest breath,
> When, his pulse failing, Passion speechless lies,
> *And Faith is kneeling by his bed of death,*
> *And Innocence is closing up his eyes.*

There is nothing in all literature more overpowering. It is lyricism, ecstasy, pure soul,

THE ENGLISH SONNET

pure poetry—what you will of high and gracious and powerful—writ down for ever; as fine as Shakespeare can be at his finest, that is to say, in the Plays and the best Sonnets; as fine and as perfect as any four lines that can be quoted out of any poet. After the *Love-Parting* we have to count to Drayton's credit, the " Phœnix " sonnet, and the sonnet on " Secricie," and " If he from heaven that filched the living fire," and " My thoughts bred up with Eagle-birds of Jove "; each a triumph in its way and each the utterance of a mouth for which " golden " is the just and sole word. There are twenty others of almost equal merit as poetry, though not so perfect as sonnets, and scarcely a sonnet in the whole collection of over a hundred which does not contain some beauty of thought or diction or some passage for the memory. Continually we come across felicities such as the following :—

> Black, pitchy night, companion of my woe,
> The urn of care, the nurse of dreary sorrow.
>
> . . . . .
>
> He framed him wings with feathers of his thought.
>
> . . . . .
>
> Thy bow half broke is piec'd with old desire,
> Her bow is beauty with a thousand strings.
>
> . . . . .

THE ROBUST

Unfainèd love in naked simple truth.

. . . . .

Yet this large room is bounded with despair.

. . . . .

Beauty sometime, in all her glory crown'd,
Passing by that clear fountain of thine eye.

. . . . .

Love, banished heaven, on earth was held in scorn,
Wandering abroad in need and beggary,
And wanting friends though of a goddess born.

There is a quality of rugged, forthright force, too, about many of the Drayton sonnets which singles them out from the "sugar'd" and "wailing" productions of the majority of his contemporaries. Indeed, while he writes almost wholly of love, and uses the word "amour'' synonymously with "sonet," h was the first of the English sonneteers to venture away from the primrose path of dalliance and compliment, and the groaning and weeping places, to engage in a little robust love-making. The following, for example, is pretty strong for an "amour":—

> Three sorts of serpents do resemble thee;
> That dangerous eye-killing cocatrice,
> Th' enchanting syren, which doth so entice,
> The weeping crocodile; these vile pernicious three.
> The basilisk his nature takes from thee,
> Who for my life in secret wait doth lie,

THE ENGLISH SONNET

> And to my heart send'st poison from thine eye :
> Thus do I feel the pain, the cause ye cannot see.
> Fair-maid no more, but *mer*-maid be thy name,
> Who with thy sweet alluring harmony
> Hast played the thief, and stol'n my heart from me,
> And, like a tyrant, mak'st my grief thy game.
> The crocodile, who, when thou hast me slaine,
> Lament'st my death with tears of thy disdaine.

Another shrewd piece, in a slyer vein, is the following, which Drayton calls "His Remedie for Love " : —

> Since to obtain thee, nothing me will stead,
> I have a med'cine that shall cure my Love,
> The powder of her heart dry'd, when she is dead,
> That gold nor honour ne'er had power to move ;
> Mix'd with her tears that ne'er her true-love crost,
> Nor at fifteen ne'er long'd to be a bride ;
> Boil'd with her sighs, on giving up the ghost,
> That for her late deceased husband died ;
> Into the same then let a woman breathe,
> That being chid, did never word reply,
> With one thrice-married's pray'rs, that did bequeath
> A legacy to stale virginity.
> If this receit hath not the pow'r to win me,
> Little I'll say, but think the Devil in me.

Sonnets such as these are, perhaps, not hugely to be admired ; but they at least serve to show that not all the early sonneteers were afflicted with the "little dog" humilities of Sidney, or disposed to take their alleged

NIMBLE DICTION

love-troubles quite so abjectly as Shakespeare feigned to do on occasion.

Drayton further furnishes us with an early example of the light or "playful" sonnet, which, of course, depends for its success on absolute polish and finish : —

> As Love and I, late harbour'd in one inn,
> With proverbs thus each other entertain,
> *In love there is not lack,* thus I begin ;
> *Fair words make fools,* replieth he again ;
> *That spares to speak, doth spare to speed,* quoth I.
> *As well,* saith he, *too forward as too slow.*
> *Fortune assists the boldest,* I reply ;
> *A hasty man,* quoth he, *ne'er wanted woe.*
> *Labour is light, where love,* quoth I, *doth pay ;*
> Saith he, *light burthen's heavy, if far borne ;*
> Quoth I, *the main lost, cast the by away :*
> You have spun a fair thread, he replies in scorn.
> And having thus a while each other thwarted,
> Fools as we met, so fools again we parted.

The neatness and deftness and keen artistry of the foregoing cannot be gainsaid. As a mere piece of nimble diction it compels respect. The management of the "quoth I's" and "saith he's" is perfect, and the "clinch" of the final couplet one of the surest we can call to mind. It has been suggested by certain critics that Drayton was a slow, stolid, clumsy sort of poet, who possessed little power of

THE ENGLISH SONNET

song apart from his themes and had to " beat out his music." Perhaps the object of art is to conceal the artist's stupidity. We must confess that so far as his sonnets are concerned, at any rate, we have read nothing of Drayton's which does not effectually conceal his alleged lack of natural executive power. And nobody in the world ever " beat out " that clinch to the " proverb " sonnet; any more than anybody in the world ever beat out—
>And Faith is kneeling by his bed of death
>And Innocence is closing up his eyes.

Although it has only an indirect bearing on our subject, we cannot resist quoting Drayton's preface to the Second Part of his *Polyolbion*, the work on which he was engaged for many years and upon which his fame as a poet is chiefly based:—

>To ANY THAT WILL READ IT. When I first undertook this Poem, or as some very skilful in this kind have pleased to term it, this Herculean labour, I was by some virtuous friends persuaded, that I should receive much comfort and encouragement therein; and for these reasons; First, that it was a new, clear, way, never before gone by any; then, that it contained all the Delicacies, Delights, and Rarities of this renowned Isle, interwoven with the Histories of the Britons, Saxons,

A PREFACE

Normans, and the later English: And further that there is scarcely any of the nobility or gentry of this land, but that he is in some way or other by his Blood interested therein. But it hath fallen out otherwise; for instead of that comfort, which my noble friends (from the freedom of their spirits) proposed as my due, I have met with barbarous ignorance, and base detraction; such a cloud hath the Devil drawn over the world's judgment, whose opinion is in few years fallen so far below all ballatry, that the lethargy is incurable: nay, some of the Stationers, that had the selling of the First Part of this Poem, because it went not so fast away in the sale, as some of their beastly and abominable trash, (a shame both to our language and nation) have either despitefully left out, or at least carelessly, neglected the Epistles to the Readers, and so have cozened the buyers with unperfected books, which these that have undertaken the Second Part, have been forced to amend in the First, for the small number that are yet remaining in their hands. And some of our outlandish, unnatural English, (I know not how otherwise to express them) stick not to say that there is nothing in this Island worth studying for, and take a great pride to be ignorant on anything thereof; for these, since they delight in their folly, I wish it may be hereditary from them to their posterity, that their children may be begg'd for fools to the fifth generation, until it may be beyond the memory of man to know that there was ever other of their families: neither can this deter

THE ENGLISH SONNET

me from going on with Scotland, if means and time do not hinder me, to perform as much as I have promised in my First Song :—

Till through the sleepy main, to *Thule* I have gone,
And seen the Frozen Isles, the cold *Deucalidon*,
Amongst whose iron rocks, grim *Saturn* yet remains
Bound in those gloomy caves with adamantine chains.

And as for those Cattle whereof I spake before, *Odi profanum vulgus, et arceo*, of which I account them, be they never so great, and so I leave them. To my friends, and the lovers of my labours, I wish all happiness.

MICHAEL DRAYTON.

We have reproduced this preface at length, because, perhaps better than any poetry might, it helps us to a picture of the plain man, of which the poet, so to say, is the child. Here again, as in the cases of Surrey and Sidney, we have no mewling, honey-lipped, sugar'd " sonneteer," but a gentleman with a temper of his own and something of a fist in which to hold the quill. The notion that poetry, and sonnets in particular, are written only by the mild-mannered, and persons in precarious health, requires to be dispelled. As a fact, great poets are not only the sanest people in the world, but physically and temperamentally the toughest, and this in spite of Keats and the

LONGEVITY

" die-young " theory. Otherwise nine-tenths of them would go under before they got their work done. And taking them on the whole sonneteers are a superior kind of poet, and saner and tougher even than the rest. Wordsworth, who wrote a greater number of sonnets than any modern poet, lived to be eighty, and Watts-Dunton, who wrote a greater number of sonnets than Swinburne, outlived him by several years, though he was born a year before him. There may be nothing in it, but for reasons of our own we like to think that there might be.

THE ENGLISH SONNET

Some atheist or vile infidel in love,
When I do speak of thy divinity,
May blaspheme thus, and say I flatter thee,
And only write my skill in verse to prove.
See miracles, ye unbelieving! see
A dumb-born Muse made to express the mind,
A cripple hand to write, yet lame by kind,
One by thy name, the other touching thee.
Blind were my eyes, till they were seen of thine,
And mine ears deaf by thy fame healèd be ;
My vices cured by virtues sprung from thee,
My hopes revived, which long in grave had lyne :
All unclean thoughts, foul spirits, cast out in me
By thy great power, and by strong faith in thee.

MICHAEL DRAYTON

How many paltry, foolish, painted things,
That now in coaches trouble every street,
Shall be forgotten, whom no poet sings,
Ere they be well wrapped in their winding-sheet?
Where I to thee eternity shall give,
When nothing else remaineth of these days,
And queens hereafter shall be glad to live
Upon the alms of thy superfluous praise;
Virgins and matrons reading these my rhymes,
Shall be so much delighted with thy story,
That they shall grieve they lived not in these times,
To have seen thee, their sex's only glory:
So shalt thou fly above the vulgar throng,
Still to survive in my immortal song.

THE ENGLISH SONNET

Dear, why should you command me to my rest
When now the night doth summon all to sleep?
Methinks this time becometh lovers best,
Night was ordained together friends to keep.
How happy are all other living things,
Which though the day disjoin by several flight,
The quiet evening yet together brings,
And each returns unto his love at night.
O thou that art so curteous unto all,
Why shouldst thou Night abuse me only thus,
That every creature to his kind dost call,
And yet 'tis thou dost only sever us.
Well could I wish it would be ever day,
If when night comes you bid me go away.

MICHAEL DRAYTON

If he from heaven that filch'd that living fire,
Condemn'd by Jove to endless torment be,
I greatly marvel how you still go free,
That far beyond Prometheus did aspire?
The fire he stole, although of heavenly kind,
Which from above he craftily did take,
Of liveless clods us living men to make,
Again bestow'd in temper of the mind.
But you broke in to heavens immortal store,
Where virtue, honour, wit, and beauty lay,
Which taking thence, you have escap'd away,
Yet stand as free as ere you did before.
But old Prometheus punish'd for his rape,
Thus poor thieves suffer, when the greater 'scape.

THE ENGLISH SONNET

In one whole world is but one Phoenix found,
A Phoenix thou, this Phoenix then alone :
By thy rare plume thy kind is easily known,
With heavenly colours dyed, with natures wonder crownd.
Heap thine own virtues, seasoned by their sun,
On heavenly top of thy divine desire ;
Then with thy beauty set the same on fire,
So by thy death thy life shall be begun.
Thy selfe, thus burned in this sacred flame,
With thine own sweetness all the heavens perfuming,
And still increasing as thou art consuming,
Shalt spring again from th' ashes of thy fame ;
And mounting up shalt to the heavens ascend :
So maist thou live, past world, past fame, past end.

MICHAEL DRAYTON

Sweet secrecy, what tongue can tell thy worth ?
What mortal pen sufficiently can praise thee ?
What curious Pencil serves to lim thee forth ?
What Muse hath power above thy height to raise thee ?
Strong lock of kindness, Closet of love's store,
Heart's Methridate, the soul's preservative;
O virtue ! which all virtues do adore,
Chief good, from whom all good things we derive.
O rare effect ! true bond of friendship's measure,
Conceit of Angels, which all wisdom teachest ;
O, richest Casket of all heavenly treasure,
In secret silence which such wonders preachest.
O purest mirror ! wherein men may see
The lively Image of Divinity.

THE ENGLISH SONNET

My thoughts bred up with Eagle-birds of Jove,
And, for their virtues I desired to know,
Upon the nest I set them forth, to prove
If they were of the Eagles kind or no :
But they no sooner saw my Sun appear,
But on her rays with gazing eyes they stood ;
Which proved my birds delighted in the air,
And that they came of this rare kingly brood.
But now their plumes, full sumd with sweet desire,
To shew their kind began to climb the skies :
Do what I could my Eaglets would aspire,
Straight mounting up to thy celestial eyes.
And thus (my fair) my thoughts away be flown,
And from my breast into thine eyes be gone.

MICHAEL DRAYTON

Since there's no help, come, let us kiss and part;
Nay, I have done : You get no more of me,
And I am glad, yea glad with all my heart,
That thus so cleanly, I myself can free,
Shake hands for ever, cancel all our Vows,
And when we meet at any time again,
Be it not seen in either of our brows,
That we one jot of former love retain.
Now at the last gasp of Love's latest breath,
When, his pulse failing, Passion speechlesse lies,
When Faith is kneeling by his bed of Death,
And Innocence is closing up his eyes,
Now if thou would'st, when all have given him over,
From Death to Life, thou might'st him yet recover.

EDMUND SPENSER

1552–1599

AT forty-two years of age the poet of *The Faerie Queen* was married to a " countrie lasse." The famous *Epithalamion* was written to celebrate the wedding, and the *Sonnets* or *Amoretti* are said to have arisen out of the courtship. We are free to admit that courtship was never more wearisomely described. From first to last the sequence, if such we must call it, is developed on lines of pure convention. " Here is a beautiful maiden. Because I am in love with her she is the most comely and beatific maiden since the Flood. But nathless she hath a hard heart, and a portly and rebellious pride. ' Fayre is she sure, yet cruell and unkind, as is a tygre, that with greediness, hunts after bloud.' " Hence eighty-eight sonnets, of level excellence as poetry, but all belauding the lady's physical charms and moral virtues, or bewailing her tygreish proclivities; and hence it comes to pass that Spenser's sonnets, despite their manifold beauties, are, on the whole, neglected. Scarcely one of them, indeed, has passed

POETRY

into what we may term the sonnet currency. There is nothing of Spenser's which the world remembers like Drayton's *Love-Parting,* or Sidney's *With how sad steps, O Moon,* or the half-dozen of Shakespeare's sonnets that are perhaps better known than anything else in literature. Yet consider the very first sonnet in the sheaf :

> Happy ye leaves ! when as those lily hands,
> Which hold my life in their dead-doing might,
> Shall handle you, and hold in love's soft bands,
> Like captives trembling at the victor's sight ;
> And happy lines ! on which with starry light,
> Those lamping eyes will deign sometimes to look,
> And read with sorrows of my dying sprite,
> Written with tears in heart's close-bleeding book.
> And happy rhymes ! bath'd in the sacred brook,
> Of Helicon, whence she derived is ;
> When ye behold that Angel's blessed book
> My soul's long-lacked food, my heaven's bliss ;
> Leaves, lines and rhymes, seek her to please alone,
> Whom if ye please, I care for other none !

He would be a churl who grumbled at such an opening, such a clean leaping right into poetry. And we do not think that there is a sonnet of the whole eighty-eight that falls below this standard, while frequently and regularly it is exceeded. How then does it happen that Spenser's sonnets are not read ? The answer is that the poet has spread over

THE ENGLISH SONNET

eighty-eight sonnets what he could easily have said in twenty. When we have learnt, as we do learn in the first dozen pieces that the lady is " fayre " and virtuous, and disdainful, we know practically all there is to know about her. At Sonnet 27 she is still " fair proud," at Sonnet 47 her looks are still but " golden hookes that from the foolish fish their baits do hide," at Sonnet 56 she is the " tygre " already mentioned, and it is not till 63 that we " do at length descry the happy shore " on which the poet hopes " ere long for to arrive." And after that, there is yet further counting and re-counting of charms, and appraisements of " blessèd lots."

> Her lips did smell like unto gillyflowers,
> Her ruddy cheeks, like unto Roses red,
> Her snowy brows, like budded Bellamoures.
> . . . . . .
> Fair bosom! fraught with virtue's richest treasure,
> The nest of love, the lodging of delight,
> The bower of bliss, the paradise of pleasure.

But even in 81 we are by no means certain of her, for while she is " fayre, when the rose in her red cheeks appears," she continues to be subject to " that cloud of pryde " which " oft doth dark her goodly light "; and right to the finish we are left in doubt as to whether

SPENSER'S RHYME-SCHEME

the " happy shore " has really been reached. So that one way or another the sequence lacks variety. It is a surfeit of the same prettily lugubrious dish, eighty-eight times repeated. Not even a poet can sit the feast through, not even a lover will be avid of the walnuts. Consequently the only way to read Spenser, the sonneteer, is to take him in places and by the separate piece, and the less we adhere to the sequence, the better are we likely to fare; the which, of course, only serves to prove what we have already said, namely, that sonnet sequences do not in the main tend to great sonnet writing. Technically, too, Spenser's sonnets suffer by their rhyme-scheme, which though in some respects melodically sounder than Sidney's, is nevertheless jarring and disappointing. Spenser's scheme for the octet runs on three sounds, thus :

a-b-a-b   b-c-b-c,

which was an attempt, of course, to combine the melody of the English octet pure and simple with the sonority of the Petrarcan octet. But though there are three rhyme sounds and the first two are rhymed as in the English octet, the ear misses the fourth, and is confused by the keeping up of *b* in the second quatrain, as well as by the couplet

THE ENGLISH SONNET

between the two. The octet, on the other hand, is always pure English, albeit the final couplet usually amounts to a subsidence—and sometimes a very bad subsidence—rather than a convincing clinch. This latter fault, which Spenser shares with Shakespeare, results largely from the cutting off of the final couplet from the sestet quatrain by a full point or its equivalent. There is obviously nothing much to be said for such " clinches " as the following :

> More sweet than Nectar, or Ambrosial meat
> Seem'd every bit which thenceforth I did eat.
>
> . . . . . .
>
> Only let her abstain from cruelty
> And do me not before my time to die.
>
> . . . . . .
>
> What then can move her ? if nor mirth nor moan
> She is no woman but a senseless stone.
>
> . . . . . .
>
> All pains are nothing in respect of this,
> All sorrows short that gain eternal bliss.
>
> . . . . . .
>
> Only behold her rare perfection
> And bless your fortunes fair election.

Of course at times a stronger effect is obtained ; as, for example :

> Enough it is for one man to sustain
> The storms, which she alone on me doth rain.

CLINCHES

or
> Yet live for ever, though against her will,
> And speak her good, though she requite it ill.

or
> Which when as Fame in her shrill trump shall thunder
> Let the world chose to envy or to wonder.

or
> Fondness it were for any being free
> To covet fetters though they golden be.

But even these lack the true force, and the impression conveyed by nearly all the "amoretti" is that the poet had either spent himself when he arrived at the end of the sestet quatrain, or believed that at this stage it was his business to allow the poetry to subside or disappear. For all that, it is to Spenser's credit that he did not confound the Petrarcan and English forms to the extent of affixing an English sestet to a Petrarcan octet; that he observed the proper break or pause between octet and sestet; that he opened the sestet with the proper "turn," and that having elaborated a form of his own he adhered to it inflexibly, as did Sidney before him and Shakespeare after him. In modern times, attempts to produce sonnets on the Spenserian model have fortunately been few and far between, and this, probably, not out of the better part of valour, but because the

THE ENGLISH SONNET

form bears its own melodic condemnation in its forehead. Spenser's dedicatory, occasional and translated sonnets scarcely call for special remark, but he is credited with the authorship of a series of blank sonnets (said to be translations from the Dutch of all languages!) which are interesting from a formal point of view, and contain some fine lines. The following, which is the concluding sonnet of the series, may be taken as an example:

> I saw new Earth, new Heaven, said Saint John,
> And lo, the sea (quod he) is now no more.
> The holy city of the Lord, from high
> Descended garnisht as a loved spouse,
> A voice that said, behold the bright abode
> Of God and men. For he shall be their God,
> And all their tears he shall wipe clean away.
> His brightness greater was than can be found;
> Square was this city and twelve gates it had,
> Each gate was of an orient perfect pearl,
> The houses gold, the pavement precious stone,
> A lovely stream, more clear than crystal is,
> Ran through the mid, sprang from triumphant rest,
> There grows life's fruit unto the Christian good.

Printed among the commendatory verses with the *Faery Queene* are two sonnets attributed to Sir Walter Raleigh. One of these, which we append, is the sonnet usually quoted to show that Milton's alleged concept of a sonnet

SIR WALTER RALEIGH

without structural pause was derived from Raleigh:

A VISION UPON THE CONCEIT OF THE *FAERY QUEENE*

Methought I saw the grave where Laura lay,
Within that temple, where the vestal flame
Was wont to burn, and passing by that way,
To see that buried dust of living fame,
Whose tomb fair love and fairer virtue kept,
All suddenly I saw the Faery Queen:
At whose approach the soul of Petrarch wept,
And from thenceforth those graces were not seen,
For they this Queen attended; in whose stead
Oblivion laid him down on Laura's hearse:
Hereat the hardest stones were seen to bleed,
And groans of buried ghosts the heavens did pierce,
Where Homer's spright did tremble all for grief,
And curst the access of that celestial thief.

Sir Sidney Lee praises these lines. In our opinion the soul of Petrarc would indeed have wept over them.

THE ENGLISH SONNET

Oft, when my spirit doth spread her bolder wings,
In mind to mount up to the purest sky;
It down is weighd with thought of earthly things,
And clogd with burden of mortality;
Where, when that soverayne beauty it doth spy,
Resembling heaven's glory in her light,
Drawn with sweet pleasures bait, it back doth fly,
And unto heaven forgets her former flight.
There my frail fancy, fed with full delight,
Doth bath in bliss, and mantleth most at ease;
Nor thinks of other heaven, but how it might
Her heart's desire with most contentment please.
Heart need not wish none other happiness,
But here on earth to have such heaven's bliss.

EDMUND SPENSER

In that proud port, which her so goodly graceth,
While her fair face she rears up to the sky,
And to the ground her eye-lids low embaseth,
Most goodly temperature ye may descry ;
Mild humblesse, mixt with awful majesty.
For, looking on the earth whence she was born,
Her mind remembreth her mortality,
Whatso is fairest shall to earth return.
But that same lofty countenance seems to scorn
Base thing, and think how she to heaven may climb :
Treading down earth as loathsome and forlorn,
That hinders heavenly thoughts with drossy slime.
Yet lowly still vouchsafe to look on me ;
Such lowliness shall make you lofty be.

THE ENGLISH SONNET

Men call you fair, and you do credit it,
For that your self you daily such do see:
But the true fair, that is the gentle wit,
And virtuous mind, is much more praisd of me:
For all the rest, how ever fair it be,
Shall turn to nought and loose that glorious hue;
But only that is permanent and free
From frail corruption, that doth flesh ensew.
That is true beauty: that doth argue you
To be divine, and born of heavenly seed;
Deriv'd from that fair Spirit, from whom all true
And perfect beauty did at first proceed:
He only fair, and what he fair hath made;
All other fair, like flowers, untimely fade.

EDMUND SPENSER

Thrice happy she ! that is so well assured
Unto her self, and settled so in heart,
That neither will for better be allured,
Nor feard with worse to any chance to start;
But, like a steady ship, doth strongly part
The raging waves, and keeps her course aright ;
Nor ought for tempest doth from it depart,
Nor ought for fairer weather's false delight.
Such self-assurance need not fear the spite
Of grudging foes, nor favour seek of friends :
But, in the stay of her own stedfast might,
Neither to one her self nor other bends.
Most happy she, that most assur'd doth rest ;
But he most happy, who such one loves best.

THE ENGLISH SONNET

Sweet is the Rose, but grows upon a brere ;
Sweet is the Juniper, but sharp his bough ;
Sweet is the Eglantine, but pricketh nere ;
Sweet is the Firbloom, but his branch is rough ;
Sweet is the Cypress, but his rind is tough ;
Sweet is the Nut, but bitter is his pill ;
Sweet is the Broom-flower, but yet sour enough ;
And sweet is Moly, but his root is ill.
So every sweet with sour is tempered still,
That maketh it be coveted the more :
For easy things, that may be got at will,
Most sorts of men do set but little store.
Why then should I accoumpt of little pain,
That endless pleasure shall unto me gain !

EDMUND SPENSER

Most glorious Lord of life, that on this day,
Didst make thy triumph over death and sin :
And, having harrowed hell, didst bring away
Captivity thence captive us to win :
This joyous day, dear Lord, with joy begin,
And grant that we for whom thou diddest die,
Being with thy dear blood clean washed from sin,
May live for ever in felicity.
And that thy love we weighing worthily,
May likewise love thee for the same again :
And for thy sake that all like dear didst buy,
With love may one another entertain.
So let us love, dear love, like as we ought,
Love is the lesson which the Lord us taught.

WILLIAM SHAKESPEARE

1564–1616

FOR a certain class of critics, poetry, like charity, begins at home. A poem, they argue, must of necessity be founded on some sort of fact. And the facts nearest to a poet's hand, and therefore likeliest to be woven into his song, are personal facts. So that if we probe deep enough, a fine poem, or for that matter a fine line, is sure to resolve itself into a species of autobiography. Or conversely, if we wish to know how the poet came by any particular thought, we can hunt up the facts of his biography and elucidate accordingly. We are unable to give chapter and verse for the following example of probing; but it is not original with us.

> There is a destiny which shapes our ends,
> Rough hew them how we will.

Here we have a considerable poetic statement. On the principle that poetry is always more or less autobiographical, we may expect

PROBING

to find in Shakespeare's life facts which will account for the manner of the statement. Ordinarily human " ends " are not likened to pieces of wood, " rough-hewn " and afterwards " shaped." What was it that prompted the poet to venture on so curious a metaphor? We know that the learned have suggested that Shakespeare's father was a butcher. And if he were a butcher, Shakespeare *père* may easily have employed his children on odd jobs about the shop—skewer-making among the number. At ten or twelve years of age, the boy Shakespeare was probably not an expert skewer-maker. He might " rough-hew " the skewers with a blunt knife; and then the elder Shakespeare would come along and with a deft stroke or two of a sharp flesher shape the ends. The child would be filled with admiration for his parent's skill and power; and pondering in after life on " destiny " and human aims and ambitions, he calls to mind the family skewer-making, and translates it into his poetry. Absurd! you will say. Quite so! But is it any more absurd than the biographical commentary which some of the exegetists continually hurl at us? In a biographical note prefixed to a selection of Francis Thompson's poems we find ourselves face to face with the following:

THE ENGLISH SONNET

A definite reminiscence of the dissecting-room at Manchester may certainly be discovered in his [Francis Thompson's] allusion (in *An Anthem of Earth*) to the heart as

> *Arras'd in purple* like the house of kings.

" A *definite* reminiscence of the dissecting-room at Manchester," mind you. What in the name of the nine sweet Muses has such a phrase as " arras'd in purple " to do with either dissecting-rooms or Manchester ? Absolutely nothing. A while back somebody published a set of war-verses called *Sons*. Up comes a by no means obscure critic with this remark : "The author is Mr. ——, who, by the way, has two sons in the war, a fact reflected in the poem." *Sons* contains the appended verse :

> We have sent them forth
>   To Christ's own rood;
> Their feet are white
>   On the fields of blood,
> And they must slake
>   Their young desire
> In wells of death
>   And pits of fire.

It happens that when the poem was written one of the author's sons was wallowing in the King's jam and doing the King's pack-drill at

THE BIOGRAPHISTS

a comfortable establishment for the training of cadets, and the other had never so much as seen a button-stick. So that the critic has accounted for *Sons* by jumping to an entirely mistaken conclusion. Of itself the matter is of no importance. But as an illustration of the dangers of the biographical method, it is instructive. When he asserts that the poem reflects something personal to its author, this critic forgets that the essential part of poetry is for all of us and not merely for one of us; a poet grapples poetically with his own experiences and his own happiness or grief in so far as he conceives them to appertain to the common lot of mankind. His whole treatment of them is directed towards making them true and actual for humanity. If he were bent on the merely personal he would keep a diary and let poetry go hang. From a diary we might, in certain circumstances, expect something like this:

April 1: Fell in love with Sarah Emily Spinks, who resides at the Holt. She is the daughter of the late Captain Spinks, of the Horse Marines, who died rich. The most beautiful woman I ever met.
April 2: She loves me.
April 3: She loves me not.
April 4: She has "accepted" me.

THE ENGLISH SONNET

April 5 : She seems a trifle too fond of Mr. Payne, the curate.

April 6 : She has gone off with Payne. Such is life!

To be particular and personal the poetry of such an affair would have to run : —

> There is no fairer maid, methinks,
> Than lovely Sarah Emily Spinks ;
>
> Her father was a man of means
> And lately in the Horse Marines ;
>
> When first I asked her to be mine
> She said she " really must decline."
>
> I spoke again on Wednesday night,
> And she replied, " Oh, well, all right ! "
>
> But late on Thursday in the lane
> I saw her kissing the Rev. Payne.
>
> On Friday, calling at the Holt,
> I found that they had " done a bolt."
>
> Oh woe, oh woe, oh woe, woe, woe,
> That Sarah Spinks should treat me so !

But the poet with a soul inside him, aching to commune with the other souls, would know better :—

> O lovelier than the loveliest star
> And statelier than the nenuphar,
> For whom my soul was all afire
> Of exaltations and desire ;

"IN MEMORIAM"

> With what a holy countenance
> Dost thou reprove my arrogance,
> And dealing forth the righteous thrust,
> Topple my joy into the dust.

This is the kind of poem that the world cuts out and puts in its pocket-book; and the poet aims to write none other. As autobiography it is not worth a row of pins. In the main it is a concealment, or if you will, a transmutation, rather than a revelation, of the facts; and he who insists that it is a revelation, or " reflection " of the Spinks affair, cannot be said to have looked into the true inwardness of poetry. The critic who described *In Memoriam* as a series of moving lyrics which " might have come straight from the full heart of an officer's widow" has been a byword these years past; but in our opinion he shot no wider of the real mark than the critic who will pretend that *In Memoriam* is a poem which depended for its essence on the actual circumstances of the friendship between Tennyson and Hallam. It is doubtful whether any poetry can be " personal " in the strict sense. Latent in the poet are certain poetic ideas which kindle and begin to find expression as soon as they are touched by the right circumstance, but whether the circumstance be personal to him-

THE ENGLISH SONNET

self or to another is a matter of little moment so far as the result is concerned. To insist upon the contrary, is to suggest that *Paradise Lost* would have been greater if Milton had actually sojourned with Eve in Paradise, or that the *Ring and the Book* is insincere poetry because Browning did not himself murder Francesca Camilla Vittoria Angela Pompilia Comparini.

All of which brings us to the question of Shakespeare's *Sonnets*. Because he is the supreme English poet, Shakespeare must always stand in that fierce light which beats upon a throne. In the last hundred years the whole searching power of criticism has been turned upon him, and the critic possessed of the biographical mind has gone over him, not only as a policeman might go over a pickpocket, but as an "X-ray" operator might go over a suspected spinal column. The results are manifest. The dramatic poet Shakespeare is quoted and admired, and read and acted and tercentenially celebrated; but it is in "the man Shakespeare" that far too many of us are sempiternally "interested." He has given us of his kingly substance, but we run after the shadow: he has said his lofty say, but we demand his "heart"; he has built up an imperishable music, but omitted to leave us a catalogue of his love

THE UNLOCKED HEART

affairs. The gods were good to him and he appears to have been reasonably good to himself. In his own time, he escaped the peepers and the botanizers, and the probability now is that they will never get him. In their rage and despair—for it is little else—they read him into the *Sonnets*, and for the matter of that even into the *Plays;* and the flat truth remains that we know just as much about him as a man of flesh and blood as ever we did ; which is admirably and gloriously little. On the autobiographical theory the *Sonnets* are his vulnerable point, the Shakespearean heel as it were. Even Dr. Furnivall, least biographically avid of all the scholars, writes of the *Sonnets* thus :—

"The sane student will be content to hold (1) *that in the Sonnets, Shakespeare did unlock his heart*—that they reveal the depths and heights of the great soul which wrote his plays ; (2) that his fair male friend and his dark, naughty, woman-love have not yet been identified, and probably never will be ; (3) that for knowledge of Shakespeare, this identification is needless, however interesting it would be. *What we want the Sonnets for, and what we get in them, is Shakespeare himself, unhid by any character in a play.*"

THE ENGLISH SONNET

Our contention is that Shakespeare did NOT unlock his heart in the *Sonnets*, any more than he may be said to have unlocked his heart in *Romeo and Juliet*, or *Hamlet*, or *Lear*, or *Othello*. We contend further that he had no " fair male friend " and no " dark, naughty woman-love " such as the *Sonnets* shadow forth and, indeed, definitely pourtray; and we deny that " what we want the sonnets for and what we get in them is Shakespeare himself, unhid by any character in a play." We are sensible that in taking up these positions we may be accused of negation for negation's sake, and that at first sight our attitude may seem utterly inconsistent with the particular theory of the sonnet which it is one of the purposes of the present work to establish. Our only course therefore is to deal with the negations *seriatim* and prove if we can not only that they are justified by the probable facts, but that they are also justified by the very sonnet theory of which they appear to be the antithesis. And now as to the negations.

The first thing we have to note in respect of the received view that the *Sonnets* are autobiographical is that the view is based very largely on something for which Shakespeare has not usually been held responsible,

THE DEDICATION

but for which in our opinion, he is responsible. We refer to the famous dedication prefixed to the folio of 1609 and purporting to be the handiwork of " T. T.," otherwise Thomas Thorpe. Everybody is familiar with the dedication : —

TO. THE. ONLIE. BEGETTER. OF.
THESE. ENSUING. SONNETS.
MR. W. H. ALL. HAPPINESSE.
AND. THAT. ETERNITIE.
PROMISED.
BY.
OUR. EVER-LIVING. POET.
WISHETH.
THE. WELL-WISHING.
ADVENTURER. IN.
SETTING.
FORTH.
T. T.

Not marble and not gilded monuments of princes shall outlive that powerful, and to our thinking, exceedingly shrewd inscription. For the autobiographists it is the groundwork and foundation of the Shakespearean sonnet literature. It is plain, they hold, that there was a " Mr. W. H." and that he was " the only begetter " of " these ensuing sonnets,"—because " T. T." says so. They assume

THE ENGLISH SONNET

that Thomas Thorpe, the "stationer," had, or took, leave and licence, to do for his poet, what poets have invariably contrived to do for themselves, namely, write their own inscriptions and arrange their own confidences, or pretended confidences, with the public. Are we to suppose that Shakespeare, the finished sonnet writer—the most finished sonnet writer of his age—was so careless of what he must have known to be a tremendous work of art, as to trust the important business of dedication to the whim and pen of his publisher? We maintain that the man who wrote those twelve lines was an artist, and not only an artist, but the best artist in dedication of his time. We can recall no dedicatory inscription in literature which is better done, or more prettily poised and balanced, and none which contains such high mounted phrases as "the onlie begetter" and "*that Eternitie promised by our ever-living poet.*" How did Thomas Thorpe come by rhetoric like that? The words we have italicized are proud enough to have walked out of the proudest of the "ensuing sonnets." They have Shakespeare written in every stroke of them, and so, as it seems to us, has the rest of the inscription. On poetical and literary grounds, which are much the safest grounds for judgment on

T. T. OR W. S.

poetical and literary things, we shall say that Shakespeare, and not "T. T.," wrote the whole inscription. As for "Mr. W. H.," what should Thomas Thorpe know or say of him? Even if there were a Mr. W. H. and assuming for the moment that he was William Herbert, Earl of Pembroke, and that his association with Shakespeare was a matter of common report, what kind of a brave man was Thomas Thorpe to set a reference to the fact in the front of a book containing sonnets such as Nos. 1 to 126? Making due allowance for everything that can be advanced to the contrary, we contend that the overwhelming probabilities are that Thomas Thorpe had just as much to do with the "Mr. W. H." reference as with the rest of the inscription, namely, nothing. How then comes it to pass that the inscription is initialled "T. T." instead of "W. S."? To poets, at any rate, the answer will be perfectly clear. A poet may boast himself in his verse, but he must not boast himself in prose. He may say "this rhyme shall live for ever" in a sonnet; but if he asserts that he is an "ever-living" or immortal poet in a dedication he runs the risk of unpleasant rebuke. Shakespeare was doubtless sick of seeing himself described as plain "Will. Shakespeare, gent," and sicker still

THE ENGLISH SONNET

of being taken by the town for a mere writer for the theatre, and of no more consequence as poet than the ruck and run of dramatic writers. He must have been conscious of his own power and genius, and not in the least averse from getting them specifically admitted. It seems to us almost certain that the *Sonnets* were, indeed, written out of a desire on the part of the author to make it evident to the world that he was something more than a successful playwright, and that he could compete with the best non-dramatic poets before him and the best poets of his period on their own ground, and even outstrip them. He is believed to have begun the sonnet series in 1597 or 1598, and they were not published till 1609. The intervening period of eleven years was the period of his prime. In those eleven years he produced for the stage *Much Ado About Nothing, As You Like It, Twelfth Night, All's Well That Ends Well, Measure for Measure, Troilus and Cressida, Julius Cæsar, Hamlet, Othello, King Lear, Macbeth, Antony and Cleopatra* and *Coriolanus.* Only *The Tempest* and *The Winter's Tale* remained to be written. From his point of view work for the stage was hack-work. He was putting into it imperishable stuff, but the fame of a playwright in those days appears to have been

MR. W. H.

just as unreal and unsatisfying as the fame of a playwright of to-day, and it is not unlikely that during the whole of this prolific time he was writing the *Sonnets* as the fit took him, but always in the faith that here was his *magnum opus*—the work which would place him among the enduring poets, as distinct from the ephemeral dramatist-poets, and make him famous for ever. And when the *Sonnets* were at length finished and ready for publication, what could be more natural than that he should desire to secure for them a "good send-off"; to put them forward in a manner which would attract attention and help to secure for him the reputation as poet to which he knew in his heart he had the fullest right? On the face of it, the dedication was the best means he could have adopted for the bringing about of this end. "To the onlie begetter of the ensuing sonnets, Mr. W. H." would excite the curiosity of the town and set the tongues of gossip wagging. And "promised by our *ever-living poet*"—not by "our admirable dramtick poet," mind you—would delight his ambitious eye, flatter his *amour propre*, and duly impress the wise world. Initialled "W. S.," "the ever-living poet" part of the performance would have been impossible; initialled "T. T." it looked

THE ENGLISH SONNET

plausible and proper and impressive, and "T. T." accordingly did duty for " W. S."

The foregoing, it will be said, is pure conjecture. We shall not deny it. But it is no more pure conjecture than that " Mr. W. H." means William Herbert, or that the dark lady of the sonnets was Mary Fitton. Moreover, it is conjecture which has all the human and poetical probabilities on its side; whereas the William Herbert-Mary Fitton conjecture, or any substitution for it, is humanly and poetically improbable. If there had been a real " Mr. W. H." the chances are that his name would either have figured in full, or been left out altogether, for in the circumstances a poet would have dedicated either handsomely or not at all. The dedication would certainly have read better without "Mr. W. H."; on the other hand, by the omission it would have lost in its power to arouse curiosity. "Mr. W. H.," we contend, was a figment, set up to provoke talk, and though it failed of its immediate purpose, inasmuch as the sonnets were not successful from a bookselling point of view, it was destined to do subsequent service for its shrewd originator, of which he may, or may not, have had a proper degree of prevision.

Let us now turn to a consideration of the

TWO LOVES

evidence of the sonnets themselves. According to the autobiographists they tell a story which is personal to the poet, the story in fact of one of his own amours. We are assured that the story is "very simple," quite an ordinary come-day-go-day episode *à trois*, in fact, and not in the least outside the range of human experience and possibility. In sonnet 144, Shakespeare is supposed to give us pretty well the whole gist of it:

> Two loves I have of comfort and despair,
> Which like two spirits do suggest me still:
> The better angel is a man right fair,
> The worser spirit a woman, color'd ill.
> To win me soon to hell, my female evil
> Tempteth my better angel from my side,
> And would corrupt my saint to be a devil,
> Wooing his purity with her foul pride.
> And whether that my angel be turned fiend
> Suspect I may, yet not directly tell;
> But being both from me, both to each friend,
> I guess one angel in another's hell:
> Yet this shall I ne'er know, but live in doubt,
> Till my bad angel fire my good one out.

That is Shakespeare's own explication, or, perhaps, more correctly, adumbration of the position. On the strength of it, and of what are held to be confirmatory passages in others of the sonnets, we are invited to believe that the dramatis personæ of the tragic tale un-

THE ENGLISH SONNET

folded were Shakespeare himself, a "rich, noble, popular," and handsome young man friend of his, and "an unworthy mistress, a dark-haired, dark-eyed Circe, skilful and unscrupulous," who held him "enthralled by the gross attraction of desire." What happened was that "on some pretext," the poet sent his rich, noble, popular young friend to the dark-eyed Circe with love messages; whereupon the dark-eyed Circe fell in love with the rich, noble, popular young friend, "wooed and won him," and left Shakespeare to "mourn the loss of both friend and mistress." In brief, William sent (Herbert?) to (Mary?) to tell her how William loved her, and (Mary?) remarked, "Why don't you speak for yourself (Herbert?)?" And in consequence of (Herbert's?) speaking up, William was left lamenting. The simplicity and ordinariness of the situation will be obvious to everybody who has not read the sonnets, but indulges a passion for Longfellow. Leaving the question of simplicity on one side for the time being, however, and presuming that Shakespeare was, in fact, thus betrayed by friend and mistress, and felt called upon to write wailful sonnets about it, what, may we reasonably suppose, would have been his method of literary procedure? It is

WHAT WOULD "A" DO?

clear that he cannot have dealt with the incidents of the plot till they had actually occurred. Without being quite so much of a prophet as, say, Mr. Israel Zangwill, he might conceivably have imagined them beforehand, in which case as a sane man he would have taken measures to prevent them from coming true. Short of such a feat of imagination—which, by the way, would have cut the whole ground of the biographists from beneath their feet—he must of necessity have had to wait, both for his impulse and his writing, till the incidents happened and were more or less within his knowledge. When the incidents did happen and pass into his knowledge, he would be able to apply them to poetical purposes, but not before. Now if *A*, a great poet, discovers that *B*, his best beloved friend, and *C*, his mistress, have made a kind of cuckold of him, his poetical attitude towards *B* (at any rate) becomes a matter for lively conjecture. Yet it seems to us that such conjecture should not be allowed to travel too far beyond the bounds of common poetical sense. When *A* sits down to unlock and unpack his heart in respect of *B*, what is likely to be his manner of approach ? Is he likely, in any conceivable circumstances, to regale rank and fleshly perfidy with this sort of thing :

THE ENGLISH SONNET

Thou that *art now* the world's fresh ornament
And only herald of the gaudy spring.

. . . . .

Thou art thy mother's glass and she in thee
Calls back the lovely April of her prime.

. . . . .

Who will believe my verse in time to come
If it were fill'd with your most high deserts?

. . . . .

If I could write the beauty of your eyes
And in fresh numbers number all your graces,
The age to come would say, " This poet lies,
Such heavenly touches ne'er touch'd earthly faces."

. . . . .

Shall I compare thee to a summer's day ?
Thou art more lovely and more temperate.

. . . . .

A woman's face with Nature's own hand painted
Hast thou, the master-mistress of my passion ;
*A woman's gentle heart, but not acquainted
With shifting change, as is false women's fashion.*

. . . . .

Lord of my love, *to whom in vassalage
Thy merit hath my duty strongly knit.*

These sugar'd commendations are taken as they arise in the first twenty-six sonnets of a series which is asserted to represent the unlocking of the heart of a poet, Shakespeare, towards a friend who has treacherously come between him-

THE DEAR FRIEND

self and the woman who holds him "enthralled by the gross attractions of desire"! In all those twenty-six sonnets there is not a word of blame, reproof, expostulation, or complaint as to wrong committed, not a suggestion of anger or jealousy, not a touch of resentment or contempt—nothing, indeed, but well and fair. What is supposed to have happened is nowhere referred to, or even so much as hinted at. The whole atmosphere is one of supreme affection, admiration, and trust. In sonnet 29 we get:

> For thy sweet love remembered such wealth brings
> That then I scorn to change my state with kings.

In 30 :—

> But if the while I think on thee (dear friend)
> All losses are restor'd, and sorrows end.

And in 38 :—

> If my slight Muse do please these curious days,
> The pain be mine, but thine shall be the praise.

In asking ourselves whether it is humanly or poetically possible that a man smarting under so grave an injury as William Herbert is said to have inflicted upon William Shakespeare could, after the event, address, not one, but twenty-six such sonnets to the author of his hurt, we have to remember that Shakespeare,

THE ENGLISH SONNET

though commonly written down as "gentle," was no amateur or dilettante either in life or letters. He had plenty of the right red and lusty blood in him, plenty of the right knowledge of the prerogatives of the human animal as well as of the human spirit, and plenty of that kind of literary vigour which makes for rough manners, but good fighting. How are we to believe that mad for Mary Fitton he could bring himself solemnly to applaud, extol, and apotheosize the "dear friend" who had treacherously supplanted him in her affections; and then, if you please, proceed to publish the proofs of his own moral turpitude among his chuckling "private friends." "The scrawled initial of the word called man," much less a flesh-and-blood poet, could not have descended to such ignominy. As a matter of fact, we think, it is safe to say that when Shakespeare set out on his sonnet writing, he was absolutely care-free so far as his affections were concerned, and the first twenty-six sonnets have no more to do with heart-unlocking in the sense insisted upon by the biographists than they have to do with the binomial theorem. We shall go further and submit that until he wrote sonnet 144—that is to say, until he came virtually to the end of his sonnet performance he had no clear

IMPERSONAL

conception of any plot or story which the sonnets should unfold, and that sonnet 144 was written out of an endeavour to give some showing of a relation to the hundred and forty-three pieces which precede it, and help the reader to imagine that he had been perusing a set tale. In other words, "the story of the sonnets," such as it is, was evolved fortuitously out of the writing and sequence of the pieces, and the sonnets were not written out of a story, personal or impersonal. Shakespeare was the best poetical story-writer of his own or any time. The whole of his work with the exception of the sonnets amounts to poetical story-writing ennobled by continual excursions into the realms of high poetry, where of necessity story ceases to exist. As surely as any other poet, Shakespeare recognised that when the pinion is at its sweep, story has to wait. He perceived that the finest poetry has no story; and in searching, as we surmise, after an achievement which should place him among the "ever-living poets" he endeavoured to throw all the knowledge of relation, of which he was a master, overboard—and give us Shakespeare the poet free of the fictional trammels into which fashion and circumstance had driven him, and were indeed to hold him to the end of his days. He

THE ENGLISH SONNET

cannot help but have been conscious of the fact that he attained his highest, as sheer poet, in short, swift flights, and when he determined to build up a work of free and high utterance his intuition told him that the sonnet form was the preordained form for his purpose. He laid mighty hands on it, and put a mighty spirit into it. He made a sonnet of his own, and continually triumphed in it. But habit is second nature, and relation would creep in. He felt that in spite of himself, he had stumbled, after sonnet 26, into the old business of story telling; and at sonnet 143 he gave up the struggle. It is as though he turned round on himself and said, " Here, after all, is a sort of tale; and it is a tale of which men will make neither fish, flesh, fowl nor good red herring; we had better devise something that will knit up the ravelment." And so we got sonnet 144, and ultimately by consequence "Mr. W. H.," and in process of time whirlwinds of pother and argument, and biography. There remains for us, however, and will ever remain, shining work; sonnets which as single pieces and in their kind are past compare. We assert that the "sequence" is of no consequence and the story, the merest accident. And as for heart-unlocking in the confessional autobiographical sense, we will have none of it.

THE MISCONSTRUCTION

We require the *Sonnets* because of the poetry they contain, and for no other reason. The best thing that could happen to them would be a rearrangement destructive of their alleged sequentiality and "story"; and as regards 1 to 126, destructive of their reference to a man. In effect the reading-mind has already accomplished these destructions for itself. Only the scholars know or read the *Sonnets* for a sequence or for a history. Ordinary people content themselves with the most beautiful and most human of them, and skip the rest. And somehow they manage to forget that 1 to 126 were not addressed to a lady. Shakespeare himself recognised that certain dangers of misconstruction attach to the group named, and he was accordingly at pains to confound evil-thinkers with a line in sonnet 20. But nearly all the most memorable pieces in the group might just as well have been addressed to Daphne as to anybody else, and this is fortunate.

Of the *Sonnets* as a literature and apart from controversy as to their origin and autobiographical interest, little requires to be said. Like all other fine poetry they praise themselves. We may note, however, that both technically and in regard to content, some of them fall very far short of the amazing stan-

THE ENGLISH SONNET

dard of excellence the work as a whole sets up. Although on what seem to us good and sufficient grounds we have advanced the conjecture that contrary to received opinion, Shakespeare was a party to their publication, and indeed expected to compass more fame by them than by his performances as dramatist, we shall not pretend that he failed of those formal and poetical lapses to which sonneteers have been so prone from the first. Genius has been described as an infinite capacity for taking pains; but in the *Sonnets*, as elsewhere, this the master genius of all time appears to have been as contemptuous of pains as a schoolboy. Since, for very good reasons, Shakespeare is seldom set up as a model for sonneteers, we shall refrain from instances. It is sufficient to note that after sonnet 144 there are three pieces (Nos. 145, 153, and 154) which are poor enough to have been written by a vastly inferior hand, and that "me," "thee," "be," "see," and so on are used for final couplet rhymes to no fewer than twenty-one sonnets, and sometimes to two in succession. Which means that one sonnet in about every seven is marred by a weak clinch.

WILLIAM SHAKESPEARE

When I do count the clock that tells the time,
And see the brave day sunk in hideous night ;
When I behold the violet past prime,
And sable curls all silver'd o'er with white ;
When lofty trees I see barren of leaves,
Which erst from heat did canopy the herd,
And summer's green all girded up in sheaves,
Borne on the bier with white and bristly beard,
Then of thy beauty do I question make,
That thou among the wastes of time must go,
Since sweets and beauties do themselves forsake
And die as fast as they see others grow ;
And nothing 'gainst Time's scythe can make defence
Save breed, to brave him when he takes thee hence.

THE ENGLISH SONNET

When, in disgrace with fortune and men's eyes,
I all alone beweep my outcast state,
And trouble deaf heaven with my bootless cries,
And look upon myself, and curse my fate,
Wishing me like to one more rich in hope,
Featur'd like him, like him with friends possess'd,
Desiring this man's art, and that man's scope,
With what I most enjoy contented least ;
Yet in these thoughts myself almost despising,
Haply I think on thee, and then my state,
Like to the lark at break of day arising
From sullen earth, sings hymns at heaven's gate :
For thy sweet love remember'd such wealth brings
That then I scorn to change my state with kings.

WILLIAM SHAKESPEARE

Devouring Time, blunt thou the lion's paws,
And make the earth devour her own sweet brood;
Pluck the keen teeth from the fierce tiger's jaws,
And burn the long-lived phœnix in her blood;
Make glad and sorry seasons as thou fleets,
And do whate'er thou wilt, swift-footed Time,
To the wide world and all her fading sweets;
But I forbid thee one most heinous crime:
O! carve not with thy hours my love's fair brow,
Nor draw no lines there with thine antique pen;
Him in thy course untainted do allow
For beauty's pattern to succeeding men.
Yet do thy worst, old Time: despite thy wrong,
My love shall in my verse ever live young.

THE ENGLISH SONNET

From you have I been absent in the spring,
When proud-pied April, dress'd in all his trim,
Hath put a spirit of youth in every thing,
That heavy Saturn laugh'd and leap'd with him.
Yet nor the lays of birds, nor the sweet smell
Of different flowers in odour and in hue,
Could make me any summer's story tell,
Or from their proud lap pluck them where they grew :
Nor did I wonder at the lily's white,
Nor praise the deep vermilion in the rose ;
They were but sweet, but figures of delight,
Drawn after you, you pattern of all those.
Yet seem'd it winter still, and, you away,
As with your shadow I with these did play.

WILLIAM SHAKESPEARE

No longer mourn for me when I am dead
Then you shall hear the surly sullen bell
Give warning to the world, that I am fled
From this vile world, with vilest worms to dwell;
Nay, if you read this line, remember not
The hand that writ it; for I love you so,
That I in your sweet thoughts would be forgot
If thinking on me then should make you woe.
O! if, I say, you look upon this verse
When I perhaps compounded am with clay,
Do not so much as my poor name rehearse,
But let your love even with my life decay;
Lest the wise world should look into your moan,
And mock you with me after I am gone.

THE ENGLISH SONNET

When in the chronicle of wasted time
I see descriptions of the fairest wights,
And beauty making beautiful old rime
In praise of ladies dead and lovely knights,
Then, in the blazon of sweet beauty's best,
Of hand, of foot, of lip, of eye, of brow,
I see their antique pen would have express'd
Even such a beauty as you master now.
So all their praises are but prophecies
Of this our time, all you prefiguring ;
And, for they look'd but with divining eyes,
They had not skill enough your worth to sing :
For we, which now behold these present days,
Have eyes to wonder, but lack tongues to praise.

WILLIAM SHAKESPEARE

Let me not to the marriage of true minds
Admit impediments. Love is not love
Which alters when it alteration finds,
Or bends with the remover to remove :—
O no ! it is an ever-fixéd mark
That looks on tempests, and is never shaken ;
It is the star to every wandering bark
Whose worth's unknown, although his height be taken.
Love's not Time's fool, though rosy lips and cheeks
Within his bending sickle's compass come ;
Love alters not with his brief hours and weeks,
But bears it out ev'n to the edge of doom :—
If this be error, and upon me proved,
I never writ, nor no man ever loved.

THE ENGLISH SONNET

So am I as the rich, whose blessed key
Can bring him to his sweet up-locked treasure,
The which he will not every hour survey,
For blunting the fine point of seldom pleasure.
Therefore are feasts so solemn and so rare,
Since, seldom coming, in the long year set,
Like stones of worth they thinly placed are,
Or captain jewels in the carcanet.
So is the time that keeps you as my chest,
Or as the wardrobe which the robe doth hide,
To make some special instant special blest,
By new unfolding his imprison'd pride.
Blessed are you, whose worthiness gives scope,
Being had, to triumph ; being lack'd, to hope.

WILLIAM SHAKESPEARE

When to the sessions of sweet silent thought
I summon up remembrance of things past,
I sigh the lack of many a thing I sought,
And with old woes new wail my dear times' waste;
Then can I drown an eye, unus'd to flow,
For precious friends hid in death's dateless night,
And weep afresh love's long since cancell'd woe,
And moan the expense of many a vanish'd sight:
Then can I grieve at grievances foregone,
And heavily from woe to woe tell o'er
The sad account of fore-bemoanèd moan,
Which I new pay as if not paid before.
But if the while I think on thee, dear friend,
All losses are restored and sorrows end.

THE ENGLISH SONNET

Not mine own fears, nor the prophetic soul
Of the wide world dreaming on things to come,
Can yet the lease of my true love control,
Suppos'd as forfeit to a confin'd doom.
The mortal moon hath her eclipse endur'd,
And the sad augurs mock their own presage ;
Incertainties now crown themselves assur'd,
And peace proclaims olives of endless age.
Now with the drops of this most balmy time
My love looks fresh, and Death to me subscribes,
Since, spite of him, I'll live in this poor rhyme,
While he insults o'er dull and speechless tribes :
And thou in this shalt find thy monument,
When tyrants' crests and tombs of brass are spent.

WILLIAM SHAKESPEARE

Poor soul, the centre of my sinful earth,
Fool'd by these rebel powers that thee array,
Why dost thou pine within and suffer dearth,
Painting thy outward walls so costly gay ?
Why so large cost, having so short a lease,
Dost thou upon thy fading mansion spend ?
Shall worms, inheritors of this excess,
Eat up thy charge ? Is this thy body's end ?
Then, soul, live thou upon thy servant's loss,
And let that pine to aggravate thy store ;
Buy terms divine in selling hours of dross ;
Within be fed, without be rich no more :
So shalt thou feed on Death, that feeds on men,
And Death once dead, there's no more dying then.

THE ENGLISH SONNET

The expense of spirit in a waste of shame
Is lust in action ; and till action, lust
Is perjur'd, murderous, bloody, full of blame,
Savage, extreme, rude, cruel, not to trust ;
Enjoy'd no sooner but despised straight ;
Past reason hunted ; and no sooner had,
Past reason hated, as a swallow'd bait,
On purpose laid to make the taker mad :
Mad in pursuit, and in possession so ;
Had, having, and in quest to have, extreme
A bliss in proof, and prov'd, a very woe ;
Before, a joy propos'd ; behind, a dream.
All this the world well knows ; yet none knows well
To shun the heaven that leads men to this hell.

JOHN MILTON

1608-1674

OF the sonnets of John Milton we have written at some length in Sections II and III of this work. Since they number but twenty-three all told, and five of them are in Italian, we may deal with them singly, in the order in which they are usually printed, pointing out their deviations from the modern sonnet law, not with a view of their belittlement as poetry, but in order that their technical blemishes may become apparent and cease to be held up as perfections worthy of imitation. Sonnet 1, called *To the Nightingale*, opens on what is now the second most hackneyed rhyme sound in the language, namely, the sound " a."

    O Nightingale that on yon bloomy *spray*.

Follow, of course, "May," "day" and "lay." Then the same vowel assonance is continued in the sestet, with "hate," "late," and "mate," while the remaining sestet rhyme is on the vowel sound "i," and the pronoun

THE ENGLISH SONNET

" I " appears twice and is used for a rhyme in the final line :

> Both them I serve and of their train am I.

Structurally, the sonnet shows a discontinuance of octet content in the middle of the seventh line. Thus in effect the octet is a line and a half short, and the break and sestet " turn " occur a line and a half before they are due. Sonnets 2, 3, 4, 5, and 6 are in the Italian ; and it is to be noted that even here Milton defies the Petrarcan rule as to the break three times out of five, and finishes each sonnet with a rhymed couplet. If we are to admit, as is contended, that this underflow, or overflow, of octet content is permissible, we may just as reasonably admit that final couplets to Petrarcan sonnets are permissible. Sonnet 7, entitled *On his being Arrived at the Age of Twenty-three*, is sound as to rhyme-scheme, though the rhyming of " show'th " and " endu'th " with " truth " and " youth " in the octet is doubtful and certainly not to be admired, and the rhyming of " high " and " eye " in the sestet is even more doubtful and less admirable. In this sonnet the true Petrarcan octet pause and sestet " turn " are properly observed. In Sonnet 8, *When the Assault was Intended to the City*, we have a perfect performance, as

A COMMENTARY

regards rhyming, structure, and break and turn alike. Sonnet 9, *To a Virtuous Young Lady*, is equally perfect, while 10, *To Lady Margaret Ley*, has only the defect of weak rhyming in the octet—"treasury," "fee," "victory," and of course "liberty." Sonnet 11, *On the Detraction which followed upon my printing certain Treatises*, perhaps ought not to be discussed as a serious poem. Its intention is plainly satirical and humorous, and in a sonnet of this kind such rhyming as "Tetrachordon," "por'd on," "word on," and "Gordon" may be excused. Here, however, we have an example of octet content running over to the end of the ninth line, with a consequent "sestet" of five lines. Sonnet 12, *On the Same*, has "liberty" rhymed with "me," "fee," and "progeny" in the octet, and "free," "see," and again "Liberty" (with a capital "L" this time) rhymed in the sestet, which, not to beat about the bush, is execrable. Here the "octet" runs to seven lines only and the "sestet" to seven lines. So that this so-called sonnet resolves itself into a fourteen-line poem, or set of verses, of two seven-line stanzas. Sonnet 13, *To Mr. H. Lawes on the Publishing of his Airs*, observes all the rules, though the rhyming of "Purgatory" with "story" in the sestet, and espe-

THE ENGLISH SONNET

cially in the last line of the sestet, ought to have been avoided. " Load " in the octet of Sonnet 14, *On the Religious Memory of Mrs. Catherine Thomson*, is not a good rhyme for " God," " trod," and " rod." The only objection we should offer in respect of Sonnet 15, *To the Lord General Fairfax*, is that the sestet contains a rhymed couplet, which is a melodic fault. The sestet of Sonnet 16, *To the Lord General Cromwell*, exhibits the defects of a rhymed couplet (lines 10 and 11), the weak rhyming of " victories " with " arise " and an unpardonable final rhymed couplet. Here again the octet is half a line too long ; but for reasons already explained, we do not count that a blemish. We take it that Sonnets 17, 18, and 19, *To Sir Henry Vane the Younger*, *On the late Massacre in Piemont*, and *On his Blindness*, will be held by the irregularists to be technically as perfect as they are indubitably fine as poetry. In the Vane sonnet, however, the distinction between octet and sestet content is almost wholly lost, and we therefore get a fourteen-line poem which is not strictly a sonnet, while in the Piemont piece the sestet " turn " really occurs in the tenth line instead of the ninth, and in the last of the three examples, the octet content is half a line short. Sonnet 20, *To Mr. Lawrence*, has

THE NEXT MILTON

rhymes in "i" carried through the octet and into the sestet—"m*i*re," "f*i*re," "re-insp*i*re," "att*i*re," and "r*i*se" and "unw*i*se," and a rhymed couplet in the sestet ; the sestet of 21, *To Cyriac Skinner*, has "w*a*y" "d*a*y," and "ord*a*ins" and "refr*a*ins" in the sestet rhyming ; in 22, *To the Same*, the sestet turn occurs in the middle of the ninth line ; and in 23, *On His Deceased Wife*, we have an octet rhymed "s*a*int," "gr*a*ve," "g*a*ve," "f*a*int," "t*a*int," "h*a*ve," and "restr*a*int," and a sestet rhymed "m*i*nd," "s*i*ght," "sh*i*ned," "del*i*ght," "incl*i*ned," and "n*i*ght."

The foregoing must not be taken as a carping upon the noble work of a poet whose refulgence goes without saying, and whose services to the English sonnet it would be impossible to overvalue ; but simply, as we have said, for a recital of a great poet's lapses from hard and fast sonnet legislation. A supreme poet, like a king, can probably do no wrong, but the assumption by lesser men that their laches are palliated because they have been indulged by eminence cannot be countenanced. When another poet of Milton's glory and power arises we will forgive him even the rhyming of "Liberty" twice in the same sonnet. Till then it is unthinkable rhyming. And if the next Milton does us the

THE ENGLISH SONNET

condescension to read these pages, he may, for the sake of the sonnet, put himself to the slight trouble of rhyming correctly. So far as the modern sonnet is concerned, " poetic license " and the appeal to offending authority should, in our opinion, be considered to have died the death.

JOHN MILTON

WHEN THE ASSAULT WAS INTENDED TO THE CITY

Captain, or Colonel, or Knight in arms,
Whose chance on these defenceless doors may seize,
If deed of honour did thee ever please,
Guard them, and him within protect from harms.
He can requite thee ; for he knows the charms
That call fame on such gentle acts as these,
And he can spread thy name o'er lands and seas,
Whatever clime the sun's bright circle warms.

Lift not thy spear against the Muses' bower :
The great Emathian conqueror bid spare
The house of Pindarus, when temple and tower
Went to the ground : and the repeated air
Of sad Electra's poet had the power
To save the Athenian walls from ruin bare.

THE ENGLISH SONNET

ON THE LATE MASSACRE IN PIEMONT

Avenge, O Lord, thy slaughter'd saints, whose bones
Lie scatter'd on the Alpine mountains cold ;
Ev'n them who kept thy truth so pure of old,
When all our fathers worshipp'd stocks and stones,
Forget not : in thy book record their groans
Who were thy sheep, and in their ancient fold
Slain by the bloody Piemontese that roll'd
Mother with infant down the rocks. Their moans
The vales redoubled to the hills, and they
To Heav'n. Their martyr'd blood and ashes sow
O'er all th' Italian fields, where still doth sway
The triple tyrant ; that from these may grow
A hundred fold, who having learn'd thy way
Early may fly the Babylonian woe.

JOHN MILTON

TO CYRIAC SKINNER

Cyriac, whose grandsire on the royal Bench
Of British Themis, with no mean applause
Pronounced and in his volumes taught our laws,
Which others at their Bar so often wrench :
To-day deep thoughts resolve with me to drench
In mirth, that after no repenting draws ;
Let Euclid rest and Archimedes pause,
And what the Swede intend and what the French.
To measure life, learn thou betimes, and know
Toward solid good what leads the nearest way ;
For other things mild Heaven a time ordains,
And disapproves that care, though wise in show,
That with superfluous burden loads the day,
And when God sends a cheerful hour, refrains.

THE ENGLISH SONNET

ON HIS BEING ARRIVED TO THE AGE OF TWENTY-THREE

How soon hath Time, the subtle thief of youth,
Stol'n on his wing my three and twentieth year!
My hasting days fly on with full career,
But my late spring no bud or blossom show'th.
Perhaps my semblance might deceive the truth,
That I to manhood am arriv'd so near,
And inward ripeness doth much less appear,
That some more timely-happy spirits indu'th.

Yet be it less or more, or soon or slow,
It shall be still in strictest measure even
To that same lot, however mean or high,
Toward which Time leads me, and the will of Heaven.
All is, if I have grace to use it so,
As ever in my great task-master's eye.

JOHN MILTON

TO A VIRTUOUS YOUNG LADY

Lady, that in the prime of earliest youth
Wisely hast shunn'd the broad way and the green,
And with those few art eminently seen,
That labour up the hill of heavenly truth,
The better part with Mary and with Ruth
Chosen thou hast; and they that overween,
And at thy growing virtues fret their spleen,
No anger find in thee, but pity and ruth.

Thy care is fix'd, and zealously attends
To fill thy odorous lamp with deeds of light,
And hope that reaps not shame. Therefore be sure
Thou, when the bridegroom with his feastful friends
Passes to bliss at the mid hour of night,
Hast gain'd thy entrance, Virgin wise and pure.

THE ENGLISH SONNET

ON THE RELIGIOUS MEMORY OF MRS. CATHERINE THOMSON

When faith and love, which parted from thee never,
Had ripen'd thy just soul to dwell with God,
Meekly thou didst resign this earthly load
Of death, call'd life ; which us from life doth sever.
Thy works, and alms, and all thy good endeavour,
Stay'd not behind, nor in the grave were trod ;
But, as Faith pointed with her golden rod,
Follow'd thee up to joy and bliss for ever.
Love led them on, and Faith, who knew them best
Thy handmaids, clad them o'er with purple beams
And azure wings, that up they flew so drest,
And spake the truth of thee on glorious themes
Before the Judge, who thenceforth bid thee rest
And drink thy fill of pure immortal streams.

JOHN MILTON

TO MR. W. H. LAWRENCE

Lawrence, of virtuous father virtuous son,
Now that the fields are dank, and ways are mire,
Where shall we sometimes meet, and by the fire
Help waste a sullen day, what may be won
From the hard season gaining ? Time will run
On smoother, till Favonius re-inspire
The frozen earth, and clothe in fresh attire
The lily and rose, that neither sow'd nor spun.
What neat repast shall feast us, light and choice,
Of Attic taste, with wine, whence we may rise
To hear the lute well touch'd, or artful voice
Warble immortal notes and Tuscan air ?
He who of those delights can judge, and spare
To interpose them oft, is not unwise.

THE ENGLISH SONNET

ON HIS BLINDNESS

When I consider how my light is spent
Ere half my days, in this dark world and wide,
And that one talent which is death to hide
Lodged with me useless, though my soul more bent
To serve therewith my Maker, and present
My true account, lest He returning chide,—
Doth God exact day-labour, light denied?
I fondly ask :—But Patience, to prevent

That murmur, soon replies ; God doth not need
Either man's work, or His own gifts : who best
Bear His mild yoke, they serve Him best : His state
Is kingly ; thousands at His bidding speed
And post o'er land and ocean without rest :—
They also serve who only stand and wait.

JOHN KEATS

1795–1821

KEATS died at twenty-five. In six years of production he put himself in the dynastic succession of the English poets. And he may be said to begin and end with a sonnet. The first poem in his first published volume is the well-known if tiresomely pretty-pretty tribute to Leigh Hunt, " Glory and loveliness have passed away." The last poem he wrote was the magnificent " Bright star, would I were steadfast as thou art," which comes very nigh perfection in the Shakespearean mould. And the pieces in the first volume (1817) included *On First Looking into Chapman's Homer*, in nearly all respects as fine a sonnet as exists in the language. Besides the two last named, we have to reckon to his glory the sonnet on the Elgin Marbles, *To Ailsa Rock*, and the sonnet to Homer, with its famous sestet quatrain :

> Aye, on the shores of darkness there is light,
> And precipices show untrodden green ;
> There is a budding morrow in midnight,
> There is a triple sight in blindness keen.

THE ENGLISH SONNET

Yet of Keats as technician, or as a contributory to the development of the modern sonnet in poetic, there is little to be said. Out of sheer flaming genius and passion he accomplished sonnet work which must rank with that of the greatest before him; but he toyed, and even frivolled, with his instrument, and had no large or sure knowledge of its nature or meaning. Tennyson said that if Keats had lived he would have been " the greatest of us all." It is certain that if he had been less addicted to Leigh Hunt he might have written many more good sonnets. In the preface to *Endymion* we get these words—from a poet who had already published *On First Looking into Chapman's Homer*:

> The imagination of a boy is healthy, and the mature imagination of a man is healthy; but there is a space of life between, in which the soul is in a ferment, the character undecided, the way of life uncertain, the ambition thick sighted; thence proceeds mawkishness, and all the thousand bitters which those men I speak of [the critics] must necessarily taste in going over the following pages.

The fact is that Keats's " mawkishness " (a very real mawkishness) arises not from himself, but by reason of his glozing vassalage to that getter-up of *Grasshopper and Cricket*

THE POET HUNT

contests, James Henry Leigh Hunt. To Keats, Hunt stood in the relation of a sort of tenth muse, and tenth muses, as we know, are usually tenth-rate. The far-famed Cockney School of English poetry was not kept by two masters, as is commonly supposed, but by one, namely, Leigh Hunt:

> He of the rose, the violet, the spring,
> *The social smile.*

On the master's judgment the pupil hung; when the master was pleased, the pupil beamed:

> And I shall ever bless my destiny,
> That in a time, when under pleasant trees,
> Pan is no longer sought, I feel a free
> A leafy luxury, seeing I could please
> With these poor offerings, a man like thee.

In one of the anthologies of the Harmsworth Professor of Literature at Cambridge, "a man like thee" is represented by *Jenny Kiss'd Me*, and by a lyric called *The Nun*, which begins thus:

> If you become a nun, dear,
>   A friar I will be;
> In any cell you run, dear,
>   Pray look behind for me.
> The roses all turn pale, too,
>   The blind will see the show.
> What! you become a nun, my dear?
>   I'll not believe it, no!

THE ENGLISH SONNET

If we remember rightly, it was Rossetti who said that poetry should be "amusing," and here, though he tears poetry up by the roots, Hunt is surely "amusing" enough to delight the whole University of Cambridge. And at such feet sate the author of *St. Agnes' Eve*—a sun; the shadow of a magnitude! Of course, Hunt, "kind Hunt," knew all about the sonnet—"that species of small poem"; and from Hunt learnt Keats. Hence,—if not the Pyramids,—*The Nile*, and *The Grasshopper and the Cricket*, and "when tired out with fun"; hence sonnets beginning, "Oh, Chatterton, how very sad thy fate," or ending:

> Meekly upon the grass, as those whose sobbings
> Were heard of none beside the mournful robins.

And hence the sonnet bastardies and tumblings from formal grace in which Keats so exasperatingly abounds. If Hunt had been a little less "kind" and a little more critical; if he had insisted that his young friend should not play fast and loose with the noble rule of Petrarc; if he had perceived that something happened in literature when the *Chapman's Homer* sonnet leapt into being; if, in brief, he had possessed even a glimmering appreciation of the fundamental tremendousness and import of the sonnet as a natural

HAMPSTEAD

poem form, we might have had from Keats more of the authentic " deep-brained " utterance, instead of so much *riddle-mi-re* and wall-paper reachings after beauty.

All of which is unprofitable crying over spilt milk, unless we take it to heart. People who hold the sonnet lightly are deficient of judgment and a danger to poetry, even though the social smile sit for ever on their handsome faces. We have no doubt in the world that it was Hunt who discouraged Keats from the pinnacles and set him standing tip-toe upon little hills, and gathering sweet peas in the suburban gardens of " poetic romance." At the top of his genius and out of the depths of his mortal tragedy he made sonnets in spite of himself. Like a sick eagle looking at the sky, he sent his soul forth to the sun which his thick-sighted mentors could see only for an inferior luminary, and in so far he achieved. But on the whole, Hunt and Hampstead held him down. Let us not forget that Hampstead still exists, and that the critical world is full of Hunts.

THE ENGLISH SONNET

ON FIRST LOOKING INTO CHAPMAN'S HOMER

Much have I travelled in the realms of gold,
And many goodly states and kingdoms seen;
Round many western islands have I been
Which bards in fealty to Apollo hold.
Oft of one wide expanse had I been told
That deep-browed Homer ruled as his demesne;
Yet did I never breathe its pure serene
Till I heard Chapman speak out loud and bold:

Then felt I like some watcher of the skies
When a new planet swims into his ken;
Or like stout Cortez, when with eagle eyes
He stared at the Pacific—and all his men
Looked at each other with a wild surmise—
Silent, upon a peak in Darien.

JOHN KEATS

ON THE ELGIN MARBLES

My spirit is too weak ; mortality
Weighs heavily on me like unwilling sleep,
And each imagined pinnacle and steep
Of Godlike hardship tells me I must die
Like a sick eagle looking at the sky.
Yet 'tis a gentle luxury to weep,
That I have not the cloudy winds to keep
Fresh for the opening of the morning's eye.

Such dim-conceivèd glories of the brain
Bring round the heart an indescribable feud ;
So do these wonders a most dizzy pain,
That mingles Grecian grandeur with the rude
Wasting of old Time—with a billowy main
A sun, a shadow of a magnitude.

THE ENGLISH SONNET

TO AILSA ROCK

Hearken, thou craggy ocean pyramid !
Give answer from thy voice, the sea-fowls' screams !
When were thy shoulders mantled in huge streams ?
When, from the sun, was thy broad forehead hid ?
How long is't since the mighty power bid
Thee heave to airy sleep from fathom dreams ?
Sleep in the lap of thunder or sunbeams,
Or, when grey clouds are thy cold cover-lid ?
Thou answer'st not, for thou art dead asleep !
Thy life is but two dead eternities—
The last in air, the former in the deep ;
First with the whales, last with the eagle-skies—
Drown'd wast thou till an earthquake made thee sleep,
Another cannot wake thy giant size.

JOHN KEATS

Bright Star! would I were steadfast as thou art—
Not in lone splendour hung aloft the night,
And watching, with eternal lids apart,
Like Nature's patient, sleepless Eremite,
The moving waters at their priest-like task
Of pure ablution round earth's human shores,
Or gazing on the new soft fallen mask
Of snow upon the mountains and the moors—
No—yet still steadfast, still unchangeable,
Pillowed upon my fair love's ripening breast
To feel for ever its soft fall and swell,
Awake for ever in a sweet unrest,
Still, still to hear her tender-taken breath,
Half-passionless, and so swoon on to death.

WILLIAM WORDSWORTH

1770-1850

To get into the technical mind of Wordsworth, particularly in its relation to the sonnet, is no difficult matter. A born sonneteer, the greatest perhaps of them all, and destined to charge the vehicle of Petrarc, Shakespeare, and Milton with new wonders, new graces, and new sublimities, his execution is the most careless in sonnet literature and his sins against the sonnet decencies steep him to the lips. From a general examination of his four hundred or so essays in this department of poetic, one might rise with the conclusion that here was a supreme poet whose genius was a sort of " something not himself " which made for sonneteering, but who was fiercely and contemptuously determined to set up for ensuing sonnet poets the highest possible standard of imperfection. Of his two sonnets on the sonnet, we have already taken cursory account. One of them appears to find acceptance as a charter whenever the sonnet is discussed. It is stuck in the forefront of the

THE SONNET SONNETS

anthologies and worn on the breasts of essayists as if it were a precious gem of the sonnet writer's art. Let us look at it closely:

> Scorn not the Sonnet; Critic, you have frowned,
> Mindless of its just honours; with this key
> Shakespeare unlocked his heart; the melody
> Of this small lute gave ease to Petrarch's wound;
> A thousand times this pipe did Tasso sound;
> With it Camoëns soothed an exile's grief;
> The Sonnet glittered a gay myrtle leaf
> Amid the cypress with which Dante crowned
> His visionary brow; a glow-worm lamp,
> It cheered mild Spenser, called from Faery-land
> To struggle through dark ways; and, when a damp
> Fell round the path of Milton, in his hand
> The thing became a trumpet, whence he blew
> Soul-animating strains—alas, too few!

Obviously the work of an easy poet or metrical emotionalist, but of a wanton, defiant, or perfunctory technician—a sonnet with a bastard Petrarcan octet (on three rhymes); without octet pause or sestet turn, and rhymed as to sestet on the Shakespearean scheme—in short, a fourteen-line poem which is strictly not a sonnet, and has a very lame ending. And all this illicity is perpetrated to the purpose that we may be bidden in the names of the masters to refrain from scorning the sonnet! Structurally, Wordsworth's second sonnet on the sonnet, "Nuns fret not at their convent's narrow room," is better; but as we

THE ENGLISH SONNET

have noted elsewhere, the view of the sonnet expressed in it cannot be considered edifying. But there is a third Wordsworthian pronouncement which the sonnet critics never quote, but which appears to us to be eminently revealing:

> A Poet!—He hath put his heart to school,
> Nor dares to move unpropp'd upon the staff
> Which Art hath lodged within his hand—must laugh
> By precept only, and shed tears by rule.
> Thy Art be Nature: the live current quaff
> And let the groveller sip his stagnant pool,
> In fear that else, when Critics grave and cool
> Have killed him, Scorn should write his epitaph.
> How does the meadow-flower its bloom unfold?
> Because the lovely little flower is free
> Down to its root, and, in that freedom bold;
> And so the grandeur of the Forest tree
> Comes not by casting in a formal mould,
> But from its *own* divine vitality.

Here in the very act and article of sonnet production the poet condemns formalism and hits upon the whole truth with regard to the sonnet, namely, that it comes not by casting in a formal mould, but from its own divine vitality. It was that divine vitality which made a sonnet writer of Wordsworth. He wrote naturally and inevitably in the sonnet form because he had a measure of genius second to that of no poet in the hierarchy, but he wanted to be free—in other words, not to take trouble over the accomplishment of form, to

DIVINE VITALITY

throw "Art" and legislation to the winds whenever the smallest difficulty presented itself; to write sonnets continually, and as continually to ignore his executive duty by the vehicle from which he could not keep his hand. We venture to assert that this "divine vitality" sonnet proves that he knew that sonnets must be written if great poetry is to be written. He knew that as often as not, when he had anything noble to say, he was impelled, and for that matter compelled, to say it in sonnet form. He knew that when the poetical breath of him was taken by some untoward realisation of grace or beauty and his spirit was illumined with the light that never was on sea or land, or stirred with emotions which lie too deep for tears, a sonnet had to result. And conversely, when he laid upon himself what he conceived to be the high tasks, he turned to the sonnet as naturally and inevitably as he turned to language and metre. He wrote "poems of the fancy," and "poems of the imagination," and "poems founded on the affections," and "poems on the naming of places," and so forth; but for the big Wordsworth, the brooding, meditative, serious, adoring, climbing soul of him, he wrote sonnets. Withal, however, he must have liberty. No putting of the heart to school

THE ENGLISH SONNET

for him ; no laughing by precept or shedding tears by rule ; no terror of rule-of-thumb critics, no fear of their critical scorn. Of course not ! And so overboard with the strict sonnet rules, especially as at times they involve labours of the file, and seem so hard of observance that nobody can hope always to observe them. We do not believe that Wordsworth ever strove for a poem in his life. He certainly never strove for a sonnet. We cannot find a single effort of his in which conscientious art, whether for art's sake or anybody else's, shows so much as a finger. Even in his finest achievements the thing is done *currente calamo*. It is the poet discharging his poetry " in tranquillity." It runs into the mould of itself, and if it comes out perfect, so much the better ; but if it come out imperfect, as nine times out of ten it does, there is no chipping or chiselling, no finishing or polishing. Furthermore, if the mould sags or leaks or is out of shape, it must sag and leak and be out of shape. The straightening or patching up of moulds is no job for the free man with the metal, some of it pure gold, and all of it golden in streaks. Only people who have no gold to run off need be particular about their moulds and careful to go over the cooled casting. We are not grumbling, but

IRREGULARISM

explaining. We are endeavouring to account for sonnets of every conceivable shape and make except the rare right one ; for sonnets with Petrarcan and pseudo-Petrarcan octets and Shakespearean or pseudo-Shakespearean sestets ; for sempiternal rhymes in " cy," " ly," and " ty "; for perpetual overflow or underflow of octet content ; for sonnets with one, two, or three sound lines in them and no more; for sonnets beginning " Jones, when from Calais southward you and I " or " ' There,' said a stripling, pointing with meet pride," or ending :

> A synod of his counsellors—give ear
> And what a pensive sage doth utter, hear !

for sonnets as full of italics as a woman's letter, and as full of capital letters as fourteen lines out of a directory. And this we do, not to asperse Wordsworth, but to warn and fortify the sonneteers of the time and the sonneteers that are to be. " It has the sanction of Wordsworth," is a justification which can be offered for literally the whole of the devisable or possible contraventions of the modern sonnet law. All of them are as easy and as artless as going to sleep, all of them are subversive not only of perfection, but of passably sound technique, and all of them are more or less winked at by the critics. In an

THE ENGLISH SONNET

introduction to the Sonnets of Sir Philip Sidney published within the last few years, we find the following words:

> It must be allowed that, all things considered, the Petrarchan type [of sonnet] with its rigid exclusion of all diffuseness, its recurrent beat, and its subtle arrangement of the sestet, whereby the rhymes are so placed as to avoid too great a sweetness, and yet are just evident enough to satisfy the ear, is best fitted to lend the sonnet that dignity and lofty economy of expression which place it in poetry as a thing apart. At the same time, dogmatism here, as in all things critical, is speedily confronted with its own folly. [*The Cambridge History of Literature*] in touching upon one of the points above mentioned, sums up the whole question in a single observation: "But the final couplet has been used so freely and to such noble ends by English writers that objection is out of place."

That is typical of virtually all the sonnet criticism extant. You put up the rule and the good reasons for the rule, and then you proceed to point out that it has been " so freely " defied, and " to such noble ends by English writers," that nobody but a dogmatist would insist upon it, and that it is " folly " so to insist.

What literature missed by the happy-go-lucky, otium-sans-dignitate methods of the

MATTHEW ARNOLD

sonneteer Wordsworth, is only too lamentably obvious. Out of four hundred pieces or thereabouts, quite three hundred and fifty are ruined by the trail of the old serpent, Slackness. One browses among them with a sick and anxious heart, finding here and there the lily amid great clumps of dock; here and there the good corn almost choked with illimitable cockle. Nobody but a poet will submit to being bored to tears by a poet; nobody but a poet will read all the sonnets of Wordsworth. And so for the only people worth thinking about, namely, the large mass of the people who read poetry, William Wordsworth's ample acres of sonnet ground can never exist. He is known by forty passable and ten perfect things who had grace enough for four hundred perfections if he would have striven.

Equally, at least, to be deplored, is the disqualifying effect of Wordsworth the technician, upon sonnet poets who have followed him. Take Matthew Arnold for example—a tremendous sonneteer deboshed by his master. With the decasyllable Arnold could write like this:

> It irk'd him to be here, he could not rest.
>   He loved each simple joy the country yields,
>   He loved his mates; but yet he could not keep,
>   For that a shadow lower'd on the fields,

THE ENGLISH SONNET

> Here with the shepherds and the silly sheep.
> Some life of men unblest
> He knew, which made him droop, and fill'd his head.
> He went; his piping took a troubled sound
> Of storms that rage outside our happy ground;
> He could not wait their passing, he is dead!
>
> So, some tempestuous morn in early June,
>   When the year's primal burst of bloom is o'er,
>   Before the roses and the longest day—
> When garden-walks, and all the grassy floor,
>   With blossoms, red and white, of fallen May,
>   And chestnut-flowers are strewn—
> So have I heard the cuckoo's parting cry,
>   From the wet field, through the vext garden-trees,
>   Come with the volleying rain and tossing breeze:
> *The bloom is gone, and with the bloom go I.*

Yet, when it comes to the sonnet, he flaunts all the illicities and all the crudities and builds a barbed wire fence round himself, apparently because he considered that what was good enough for Wordsworth was good enough for Arnold. Here are his lines, " Written in Butler's Sermons ":

> Affections, Instincts, Principles, and Powers,
> Impulse and Reason, Freedom and Control—
> So men, unravelling God's harmonious whole,
> Rend in a thousand shreds this life of ours.
> Vain labour! Deep and broad, where none may see,
> Spring the foundations of the shadowy throne
> Where man's one Nature, queen-like, sits alone,
> Centred in a majestic unity,

ETERNITY

And rays her powers, like sister islands, seen
Linking their coral arms under the sea :
Or cluster'd peaks, with plunging gulfs between
Spann'd by aërial arches, all of gold ;
Whereo'er the chariot wheels of Life are roll'd
In cloudy circles, to eternity.

Octet on four rhymes, neither Petrarcan nor Shakespearean ; sestet with a couplet in it ; " see," " unity," " sea," " eternity " rhymed together ! And " eternity " for the last word in the last line ! One might be forgiven for thinking that eternity had been invented not only to be the puzzle of finite souls, but the undoing of careless sonneteers. Having thus scrawled himself on the fly-leaf of Butler's Sermons, Arnold writes another lumpy " sonnet " in Emerson's Essays and rhymes cheerfully " by " and " incredulity," " full " and " beautiful " and " free " and " mockery " — " mockery," of course, being the last word in the fourteenth line. In further efforts he rhymes " high " and " necessity," " thee," " enmity," " tranquillity " and " rivalry," " Necropolis " and " his," " free," " majesty," " mortality " and " sea " (in the famous Shakespeare sonnet which has a double bar sinister in the octet), " thee " and " impossibility," " eyes " and " sophistries," " are " and " share," " thee " and " sea," " vul-

THE ENGLISH SONNET

garity " and " imbecility " (in a close rhyme), " be," " me," " Italy " and " sea " and so on and so forth *ad nauseam*. The later " Wordsworthians " have been similarly, if not quite so flagrantly, careful to reproduce and perpetuate the greater poet's faults, and the only sonnet Mr. Thomas Hardy has seen fit to include in his late volume of " Selected Poems " offers us the everlasting gin-mule rhyming — " sea," " serenity," " symmetry," " misery."

If we took the trouble we could cite literal hundreds of additional instances in point. A collection of only nineteen otherwise excellent sonnets published recently has the following rhymes : " me," " memory," " colloquy," " thee " ; " hostility," " me," " knee," " hypocrisy " ; " Italy," " memory," " be," " minstrelsy " ; " loyalty," " me " ; " ecstasy," " eternity," " grudgingly," " immortality " ; " thee," " symmetry," " sea," " immortality " ; " curiosity," " thee," " tree," " flee " ; and " inconstancy," " thee." Thus is poetical indolence justified of her children, and thus is the writing of sonnets reduced to a species of kindergarten entertainment. Of course we must still love and be thankful for these easy and inspired purveyors of easy and uninspired rhyming; but how much more closely we could have loved them, and how

ITERATION

much more thankful could we have been for them, if they had toiled a little as well as spun. And lest there should be any misunderstanding, let us hasten to note the obvious, namely, that there is nothing wrong with " thee," " me," " be," " see," " free," " knee," " we," or for that matter even " fiddle-de-dee," and still less with " majesty," " constancy," " immortality," " minstrelsy," " eternity," " ecstasy," and if you like " grudgingly "; all of which are good words and meet to be used in any poetry. The fault lies not in their use as words, but in their persistent, inveterate, and iterated use as rhymes, and particularly in the use of the polysyllables as final sestet rhymes.

To get back to Wordsworth, whom we hold to be the father of this and pretty well every other modern sonnetal abuse, we must not dismiss him in any but the most reverent spirit. Emotionally he lifted the sonnet to heights never before attained, and sounded with it depths never before plumbed. He made it an affair of the intellect and the brooding spirit as well as of the fancy and the passions. In his hand the thing became an ecstasy as well as a trumpet, a vision and a tenderness as well as an austerity. And as it is by these qualities of rapture, vision, and tenderness the English

THE ENGLISH SONNET

poetry exceeds and outstrips and outsoars all other poetry, we may say that it was Wordsworth who gave to the modern English sonnet the special qualities that make it English. The modern English sonnet as we conceive of it and hope for it, began with him, and in its glories, achieved and to come, he must always have part.

WILLIAM WORDSWORTH

O Friend, I know not which way I must look
For comfort, being, as I am, opprest,
To think that now our Life is only drest
For show ; mean handy-work of craftsman, cook,
Or groom !—We must run glittering like a Brook
In the open sunshine, or we are unblest :
The wealthiest man among us is the best
No grandeur now in nature or in book

Delights us. Rapine, avarice, expense,
This is idolatry ; and these we adore :
Plain living and high thinking are no more
The homely beauty of the good old cause
Is gone : our peace, our fearful innocence,
And pure religion breathing household laws.

THE ENGLISH SONNET

Fair Star of Evening, Splendour of the West,
Star of my country !—on the horizon's brink
Thou hangest, stooping, as might seem, to sink
On England's bosom : yet well pleased to rest,
Meanwhile, and be to her a glorious crest
Conspicuous to the Nations. Thou, I think,
Should'st be my Country's emblem ; and should'st wink,
Bright Star ! with laughter on her banners, drest

In thy fresh beauty. There ! that dusky spot
Beneath thee, it is England ; there it lies.
Blessings be on you both ! one hope, one lot,
One life, one glory ! I with many a fear
For my dear Country, many heartfelt sighs,
Among men who do not love her, linger here.

WILLIAM WORDSWORTH

The World is too much with us ; late and soon,
Getting and spending, we lay waste our powers ;
Little we see in Nature that is ours ;
We have given our hearts away, a sordid boon !
This Sea that bares her bosom to the moon,
The winds that will be howling at all hours
And are up-gather'd now like sleeping flowers,
For this, for everything, we are out of tune ;

It moves us not.—Great God ! I'd rather be
A Pagan suckled in a creed outworn,—
So might I, standing on this pleasant lea,
Have glimpses that would make me less forlorn ;
Have sight of Proteus rising from the sea ;
Or hear old Triton blow his wreathed horn.

THE ENGLISH SONNET

MILTON

Milton, thou shouldst be living at this hour :
England hath need of thee : she is a fen
Of stagnant waters : altar, sword, and pen,
Fireside, the heroic wealth of hall and bower,
Have forfeited their ancient English dower
Of inward happiness. We are selfish men ;
Oh ! raise us up, return to us again ;
And give us manners, virtue, freedom, power.

Thy soul was like a Star, and dwelt apart :
Thou hadst a voice whose sound was like the sea :
Pure as the naked heavens, majestic, free,
So didst thou travel on life's common way,
In cheerful godliness ; and yet thy heart
The lowliest duties on herself did lay.

WILLIAM WORDSWORTH

When I have borne in memory what has tamed
Great nations ; how ennobling thoughts depart
When men change swords for ledgers, and desert
The student's bower for gold,—some fears unnamed,
I had, my Country !—am I to be blamed ?
But when I think of thee, and what thou art,
Verily, in the bottom of my heart
Of those unfilial fears I am ashamed.

For dearly must we prize thee ; we who find
In thee a bulwark of the cause of men ;
And I by my affection was beguiled :
What wonder if a Poet now and then,
Among the many movements of his mind,
Felt for thee as a lover or a child !

THE ENGLISH SONNET

AFTER-THOUGHT

I thought of Thee, my partner and my guide,
As being past away.—Vain sympathies !
For, backward, Duddon ! as I cast my eyes,
I see what was, and is, and will abide ;
Still glides the stream and shall for ever glide ;
The Form remains, the Function never dies ;
While we the brave, the mighty, and the wise,
We men, who in our morn of youth defied
The elements, must vanish ;—be it so !

Enough, if something from our hands have power
To live, and act, and serve the future hour ;
And if, as toward the silent land we go,
Through love, through hope, and faith's transcendent dower,
We feel that we are greater than we know.

WILLIAM WORDSWORTH

TO TOUSSAINT L'OUVERTURE

Toussaint, thou most unhappy man of men!
Whether the whistling rustic tend his plough
Within thy hearing, or thy head be now
Pillowed in some deep dungeon's carless den;—
O miserable Chieftain! where and when
Wilt thou find patience? Yet die not; do thou
Wear rather in thy bonds a cheerful brow:
Though fallen Thyself, never to rise again,

Live, and take comfort. Thou hast left behind
Powers that will work for thee; air, earth, and skies;
There's not a breathing of the common wind
That will forget thee; thou hast great allies;
Thy friends are exultations, agonies,
And love, and Man's unconquerable mind.

THE ENGLISH SONNET

COMPOSED UPON WESTMINSTER BRIDGE

Earth has not anything to show more fair :
Dull would he be of soul who could pass by
A sight so touching in its majesty :
This city now doth like a garment wear
The beauty of the morning ; silent, bare,
Ships, towers, domes, theatres, and temples lie
Open unto the fields, and to the sky :
All bright and glittering in the smokeless air.

Never did sun more beautifully steep
In his first splendour valley, rock, or hill ;
Ne'er saw I, never felt, a calm so deep !
The river glideth at his own sweet will :
Dear God ! the very houses seem asleep ;
And all that mighty heart is lying still !

WILLIAM WORDSWORTH

It is a beauteous Evening, calm and free ;
The holy time is quiet as a Nun
Breathless with adoration ; the broad sun
Is sinking down in its tranquillity ;
The gentleness of heaven is on the sea ;
Listen ! the mighty Being is awake,
And doth with his eternal motion make
A sound like thunder—everlastingly.

Dear Child ! dear Girl ! that walkest with me here,
If thou appear'st untouched by solemn thought,
Thy nature is not therefore less divine :
Thou liest in Abraham's bosom all the year ;
And worshipp'st at the Temple's inner shrine,
God being with thee when we know it not.

CONTEMPORARY

THE sonneteers since Wordsworth are a notable company, including pretty well every great name in poetry, to say nothing of a wilderness of small ones. We shall deal with them particularly, in a future volume. For the purpose of illustrating the contemporary sonnet in its perfected aspects we have chosen only three pieces. These we consider to be in the sonnetal succession, though one of them is by a late Poet Laureate, and villainously rhymed, and the second has a close rhyme in the sestet. It will be noted that the third piece, Mrs. Meynell's *Renouncement*, has a feminine "never, never" and four " thees " in the octet with the curiously otiose "difficult day" in the first line of the sestet. Despite these shortcomings, however, we must place it side by side with the *Love Parting* of Drayton, and Wordsworth's Westminster Bridge sonnet and " It is a beauteous evening calm and free." That is to say, it is one of the four greatest sonnets of pure emotion in English.

Of the received, approved, and established

CONTEMPORARY

contemporary sonneteers, Rossetti, Tennyson-Turner, and Mrs. Browning, we are unable to offer a high estimate. Their poetical parts are not in question. Their sonnets, as sonnets, break the heart, and fail of the compensating glows which would move us to forgiveness. Rossetti was the father of the sonnetal mechanician, Tennyson-Turner was the father of "Letty's Globe" and the pretty prettinesses, and Mrs. Browning was the mother of hyper-sentiment. All three have a sort of life in them which may keep them going at the bookshops and find them places in the anthologies. But they lack wing and never tasted breath.

For the rest: Tennyson killed himself as sonneteer when he took to Malory; in the hand of Swinburne the thing became a dedication and no great matter at that; Robert Browning managed to tell us in fourteen lines why he was a Liberal, and Matthew Arnold, with some of the power of Milton and Wordsworth, anticipated the technique of Mr. Justice Darling.

ALFRED AUSTIN

Within the hollow silence of the night
I lay awake and listened. I could hear
Planet with punctual planet chiming clear,
And unto star star cadencing aright.
Nor these alone : cloistered from deafening sight,
All things that are made music to my ear :
Hushed woods, dumb caves, and many a soundless mere,
With Arctic mains in rigid sleep locked tight.

But ever with this chant from shore and sea,
From singing constellation, humming thought,
And Life through Time's stops blowing variously,
A melancholy undertone was wrought ;
And from its boundless prison-house I caught
The awful wail of lone Eternity.

GEORGE MEREDITH

On a starred night Prince Lucifer uprose.
Tired of his dark dominion swung the fiend
Above the rolling ball in cloud part screened,
Where sinners hugged their spectre of repose.
Poor prey to his hot fit of pride were those.
And now upon his western wing he leaned,
Now his huge bulk o'er Africa careened,
Now the black planet shadowed Arctic snows.

Soaring through wider zones that pricked his scars
With memory of the old revolt from Awe,
He reached a middle height, and at the stars,
Which are the brain of heaven, he looked, and sank.
Around the ancient track marched, rank on rank,
The army of unalterable law.

ALICE MEYNELL

RENOUNCEMENT

I must not think of thee ; and, tired yet strong,
I shun the love that lurks in all delight—
The love of thee—and in the blue Heaven's height,
And in the dearest passage of a song.
Oh, just beyond the sweetest thoughts that throng
This breast, the thought of thee waits hidden yet bright ;
But it must never, never come in sight ;
I must stop short of thee the whole day long.

But when sleep comes to close each difficult day,
When night gives pause to the long watch I keep,
And all my bonds I needs must loose apart,
Must doff my will as raiment laid away,—
With the first dream that comes with the first sleep
I run, I run, I am gathered to thy heart.